MW00442403

The Supercars

John Lamm

MBI Publishing Company

This edition published in 2002 by
MBI Publishing Company,
Galtier Plaza, Suite 200, 380 Jackson Street,
St. Paul, MN 55101-3885 USA

© John Lamm, 2001, 2002

All rights reserved. With the exception of quoting
brief passages for the purposes of review, no part
of this publication may be reproduced without
prior written permission from the Publisher.

The information in this book is true and complete
to the best of our knowledge. All recommendations
are made without any guarantee on the part of the
author or Publisher, who also disclaim any liability
incurred in connection with the use of this data or
specific details.

We recognize that some words, model names
and designations, for example, mentioned herein
are the property of the trademark holder. We use
them for identification purposes only. This is not
an official publication.

MBI Publishing Company books are also available
at discounts in bulk quantity for industrial or
sales-promotional use. For details write to Special
Sales Manager at Motorbooks International
Wholesalers & Distributors, Galtier Plaza,
Suite 200, 380 Jackson Street, St. Paul, MN
55101-3885 USA.

Library of Congress Cataloging-in-Publication
Data Available

ISBN 0-7603-1488-8

Printed in China

CONTENTS

ACKNOWLEDGMENTS

It would take almost another book to acknowledge all those who have helped—knowingly or otherwise—with this book, so I can only skim the cream off the top. Thanks to people such as Harry Calton at Aston Martin, Michael Schimpke at Porsche, and Ferrari's Antonio Ghini. Reeves Callaway, Steve Saleen, and Louis Ruf, who assisted with the cars that bear their name. Nissan's Miki Kurosu, Mercedes-Benz's Craig Morningstar, probably a half dozen staffers with the Dodge public relations crew, and an equal number at Lamborghini. Bill Donnelly, who was then with Jaguar. Horacio Pagani and Mike Perry at Pagani.

Thanks also to Tom Bryant, Editor-in-Chief of *Road & Track*, for sending me on the assignments that led to the photography and stories included here. To the magazine's art director, Richard Baron, who has always made my photography look better than it really is. And my old friend, Alan Rosenberg, who did the photos of the Ruf CTR-2 and takes perhaps the most delicious food photos in the world.

I cannot forget the patience of MBI Publishing Company editors Zack Miller, Sara Perfetti, and, above all, Paul Johnson, as well as the understanding of my dear wife, Scheri, and our sweet daughter, Holly, for those hours when I disappeared to work on this book.

And to all the exotic car fans whose enthusiasm for these great automobiles never slackens.

—*John Lamm*

INTRODUCTION

He did not have to ask twice.

When Giuseppe Grecco, managing director of Lamborghini, asked, "Are you going to drive now?" I laid down my camera and slipped into the seat of the 6.0-liter Diablo VT. We were at a small track just south of Milan, Italy, with a Ferrari Formula 1 car screaming through a test in the background. Down with the Diablo's door, into first gear, and off we go with all the speed and discretion one can muster in someone else's quarter-million-dollar automobile.

A tough business, but someone has to do it.

When heading out in a new exotic car, I often recall the first one I had the chance to drive. It was a red Ferrari Daytona and we were on one of the well-known canyon roads north of Los Angeles. In the 30 years since then, recessions, fuel shortages, and ever-tightening emissions and safety regulations all threatened to do away with supercars, but never succeeded . . . and for the best of reasons.

Whether called exotic cars, supercars, or wondercars, they all have that same effect. Owners and drivers treat them like honored guests, and car fans go weak in the knees when a Lamborghini Diablo, a Callaway Corvette, a Ruf Porsche, or just about any Ferrari cruises by—it's a natural reaction from anyone who loves automobiles because these are the most exciting, blood-stirring machines in the world.

What makes an exotic car? There are no hard-and-fast rules, but they must be fast: quick to 60 miles per hour, a top speed of 150 miles per hour or more, and able to make tracks along a twisty road at an impressive rate. As a result of all that speed, excellent brakes are also required.

Exotic automobiles must look as fast as they go. To some eyes that beauty means the body must be clean and aero sleek. Others prefer their supercars festooned with wings and spoilers. Either can be correct as long as the car tickles your heartstrings.

It doesn't hurt if a supercar is made in an exotic-sounding place such as Maranello, Italy; Zuffenhausen, Germany; or Newport Pagnell, England; though Bowling Green, Kentucky, and Irvine, California, also qualify if the car is good enough.

Whether Italian, German, British, Japanese, or American, these wondercars tend to be low, so you must step over and down to get in. The seats are usually firm and supportive, so you easily settle in, hook up the seat belts, and adjust the cockpit to your size. The instruments are legible and not far off your down-the-road sight lines. Controls like the steering wheel, shifter, and pedals are logically laid out and have a firm, positive feel to them.

Whether you start the car with the key or a button, it is instantly obvious there's big stuff powering the car, be it the throaty, almost-threatening rumble of a V-8 or the smooth strength of a V-12. Into the first of its many gears, bury the throttle, and the ride begins . . . and it's like no other on earth, whether you are rocketing down a strip of empty German autobahn, knocking down hot laps on an Italian test track, or snaking along a California mountainside highway.

We dare you to not smile.

Exotic cars are not perfect automobiles. Many have only limited visibility to the rear. Some are difficult to clamber into and even tougher to exit. Parallel parking can be a chore. There was a time when they were mechanically fussy, earning exotic machines the label "weekend cars" because they were not dependable, but modern electronics have done away with that down side.

Besides, the exterior styling will steal your practical heart, whether you are an owner, someone by the side of the road, or a photographer caressing the car's shapes and details with a camera as the sun melts into that sweet sunset light.

I can also attest to the fact exotic cars make a wonderful ride: topping 212 miles per hour in a Ruf while riding with 1961 World Drivers' Champion Phil Hill as he deftly catches a side-wind-induced slip; wondering if the legendary Maserati test driver Guerino Bertocchi has noticed how quickly we are closing in on the car ahead during a high-speed early morning Autostrada test run; admiring the steering wheel movements and footwork of rally champion Sandro Munari as he kicks a Lamborghini Countach sideways on a tight Italian mountain road.

The ride of your life in the most exciting cars of our lifetime.

chapter 1

GERMANY

Mention the words "exotic cars" and "Germany" and the words that tend to follow are "Porsche" and "turbo." Few automobiles have captured the imagination of performance-car lovers around the world like the many forms of turbocharged Porsches. Just saying "959" is enough.

Recently, other German automakers have ventured into the supercar business. Mercedes is prepping the SLR. BMW has opened the door with its Z8 sports car. Volkswagen is even getting into the exotic car biz via ownership of Lamborghini and Bugatti.

For years, however, there has been an exotic automotive subculture in Germany built around tuners. Take a walk through the annual Geneva Auto Show and you'll see them; companies with such names as Brabus, Renntech, Gemballa, and Alpina will create any outrageous one-off German hot rod you could dream up. Want a Mercedes V-12 stuffed into your E-Class? A BMW V-12 in that 3-Series? They'll do it . . . for a healthy price.

Germany has created a few purpose-built supercars, such as the Isdera Imperator and the Dauer 962, but the long-term success of German high-performance cars has been with the tuners who start with stock Mercedes, BMW, Porsche, Opel, or Audi parts and, well, hot rod them.

That's how AMG—provider of Mercedes' high-performance engines—got started, working a backdoor relationship with the automaker for years before it bought the nearby speed shop. BMW had a similar relationship with Alpina, though the two have never grown as close as Mercedes and AMG. Louis Ruf's tuning of Porsches is so extreme his cars are no longer Porsches, but registered as Rufs. And now Porsche has expanded its custom program, willing to build special versions of its cars for customers.

If there is one thing that stands out among the top-line German tuners—as with the country's automakers—it is the superb quality of their work. Between German pride in workmanship, certain laws, and the fact that the cars can be exercised at high, unforgiving speeds on the autobahn, German supercars tend to be among the best made in the world.

RUF CTR-2

Bury the throttle of a silver Ruf CTR-2 and the car leaps forward. Turbochargers instantly spool up, and you can almost feel the horsepower and torque curves go to near vertical. Snatch second gear. Wham, you're on a run that's going to get you to 100 miles per hour in just 7.9 seconds, and on this highly crowned back road in rural Germany you find yourself adding small steering corrections to keep the car pointed straight ahead. And yet for all this speed and fury, the CTR-2 is as well behaved as it is quick.

That's Louis Ruf's way.

In the small village of Pfaffenhausen, Germany, about an hour's drive west of Munich, Louis Ruf creates his own, special breed of automobiles. At first look, you would be justified

in thinking he makes highly tuned Porsches. His cars certainly appear to be just that, but if you search the car you won't find any Porsche nameplates or chassis tags. Ruf and his highly trained crew so completely rework the cars that they replace the Porsche chassis numbers with their own, because officially Ruf is a German automaker . . . the country's smallest, perhaps, but an automaker nonetheless.

Road & Track discovered Ruf's potential many years ago, and invited him to bring a car to its first World's Fastest Cars roundup. It was 1987 and Louis Ruf showed up at Volkswagen's impressive Erha-Lessien test track near Wolfsburg, Germany, with a car nicknamed Yellow Bird. The "sleeper" appeared deceptively simple compared to the other super

They may look like Porsches, but according to the German government, the cars built by Louis Ruf are called "Ruf" right on their serial number plates. Although they may begin as 911s, by the time Ruf has finished, the cars—such as this CTR-2—are so highly modified that they are reclassified. *Allan Rosenberg*

Opposite: **Yes, those are the basic design lines of the 911, but the front and rear bumpers and the engine cover are all new, made to Ruf's exacting standards. Louis Ruf also adds 19-inch forged magnesium road wheels of his own design.** *Allan Rosenberg*

A chunk of the development time goes into the chassis, with the springs, shock absorbers, and anti-roll bars all being firmed up to match the higher performance of the car. Inside those huge alloy wheels are brakes commensurate with the CTR-2's high performance. *Allan Rosenberg*

Porsches. For one thing, Ruf prefers to start his rebuild process with non-Turbo-fender-flare Porsches because they are narrower, with less frontal area. Since top speed was the issue, the car was wingless. And it was very fast, winning the competition at 211 miles per hour.

From the beginning, Ruf's specialty has been engines. He starts by disassembling the latest Porsche flat-six and meticulously rebuilding it like a race-prepped engine. In the case of the CTR-2 (based on the last-generation 911) he adds larger KKK turbochargers and ups the boost from 13.1 to 16.0 psi. Engine-control electronics are remapped for performance, though the engine will pass all necessary national antipollution laws. Helping on the low-emission front are twin steel catalytic converters plumbed into a Ruf-developed exhaust system. The result? Some 520 horsepower and 505 lb-ft of torque.

Ruf has been known to design gearboxes for his own cars, usually adding a gear, although these days he stays with the Porsche six-speed manual. He also offers the option of either rear- or four-wheel drive, the latter a good idea when you're pasting 520 horsepower to the pavement.

While the need for ultimate velocity has kept many Ruf bodies quite simple for top speed, he will also go after downforce with specially created, beautifully finished bodywork for models like the CTR-2. Front and rear spoilers are calculated to increase downforce, while internal ducting vents intercooler heat away from the car.

To match the car's higher performance, a Ruf chassis receives the same detail attention as the engine and body. Shock absorbers, springs, struts, and anti–roll bars are all firmed and reworked to balance the chassis with the mega-horsepower. Add

The real genius in Louis Ruf's cars is in the engine. Ruf's engine builders start with the Porsche flat-six and, among other things, bump up the turbo pressure to 16.0 psi, remap the electronics, add high-speed catalytic converters, and come away with 520 horsepower and 505 lb-ft of torque. *Allan Rosenberg*

a set of Ruf's unique forged magnesium 19-inch wheels fitted with very low, wide Z-rated tires and you have a platform firm enough to handle the power without being overly rough or rumbly in ride.

The keep-it-simple approach continues inside the car. You will never mistake a Ruf interior for a monk's cell, but it will not be overdone or gaudy. You'll find the air conditioning and sound system needed to cope with warm days and long distances, but you might also find special lightweight door panels with pull-strap door openers in place of the heavy handle mechanism. Ruf-designed seats have less weight than Porsche's and added lateral support. As custom-made cars, Rufs can be ordered with just about any option from a sunroof to, heck, a beverage cooler, though that would be missing the point of the Pfaffenhausen cars.

The point is speed—both terminal velocity and getting there as quickly and as safely as possible.

That's Louis Ruf's way.

RUF CTR-2

Base price: $280,000

Specifications
General

Layout	rear engine, rear drive
Wheelbase (in.)	89.4
Overall length (in.)	168.9
Overall width (in.)	68.3
Overall height (in.)	51.2
Curb weight (lbs.)	3,045

Drivetrain

Engine	twin-turbocharged sohc 12-valve flat-six
Bore x stroke (mm)	100.0x76.4
Displacement (cc)	3,600
Horsepower	520 bhp @ 5,800 rpm
Torque	505 lb-ft @ 4,800 rpm
Transmission	six-speed manual

Body & Chassis

Front suspension	MacPherson struts, lower A-arms, coil springs, tube shocks, anti-roll bar
Rear suspension	twin lateral links, lower A-arms, toe links, coil springs, tube shocks, anti-roll bar
Steering	rack and pinion, variable power assist
Brakes	14.0-inch carbon-fiber discs
Wheels	19x8-1/2 front, 19x10 rear
Tires	245/35ZR-19 front, 285/30ZR-19 rear

Performance

0 to 60 mph	3.6 seconds
Top speed	217 mph (estimated)

PORSCHE 959

It seemed to take forever for the traffic to clear. We were headed north from Porsche's factory in Zuffenhausen, Germany—a suburb of Stuttgart—on the autobahn in a Porsche 959, and for the first time I had the controls. But when would the line of cars thin and fade to the right so I could safely open up Porsche's supercar?

At this point all we were opening up were eyeballs that stared at the 959. The super Porsche stood out in autobahn traffic like a super hero among everyday wimps: ultra aggressive with its swoopy tail spoiler, a broad stance resting on squat tires, wide cooling slots traced across its nose, and, in our case, bright red paint.

The immediate impression you get when sitting in the driver's seat of a 959 is that you aren't driving a car so much as piloting a system. Perhaps the impression stems from the way the cockpit's tall center tunnel makes you feel compartmentalized behind the wheel, or maybe it's from the added levers and controls of the four-wheel-drive system, or maybe it's because you know you have control over so many variables . . . a great sense of command.

Based on a show car called the Gruppe B, the 959 caused a sensation when it was unveiled in 1987. Many of the car's styling cues, such as the front air inlets, were used on production Porsches for several generations after the 959.

There is something slightly space age about the 959 cockpit, such as the many controls that allow you to command systems including the four-wheel drive. The basics of the design, however, come from the stock 911 and can be seen in the dashboard layout and the seats.

It all began when the 911 Turbo was reworked to adhere to international Group B racing rules. Porsche unveiled a show-car version at the 1983 Frankfurt Auto Show with the name Gruppe B.

Group B racing rules dictated engine displacement-to-car weight scales that restricted the 959's flat-six powerplant to 2.9 liters. The engine was fitted with water-cooled, four-valve-per-cylinder heads and a pair of KKK turbochargers. To aid low-speed torque and response, the exhaust is first routed to one turbo, then to the second as rpm increases. This means a secondary, rushing kick-in-the-back around 4,200 rpm in each of the six gears as the engine winds to 450 horsepower at 6,500 rpm.

Great as the 959's engine might be, however, its main attraction is how that power gets to the ground: all-wheel drive. A steering column stalk allows the driver to choose one of four settings:

Dry, Wet, Snow, or Traction. Normally you'd use the first two, which vary the amount of power going to the front and rear wheels from the normal 40 front/60 rear to 20/80 under hard acceleration. The Snow setting holds the split at 40/60, while Traction then locks the rear and center differentials for maximum grip.

But there's more.

A normal-production 959 has amenities such as air conditioning and electric window lifts, plus an adjustable suspension. Normal ride height is 4.7 inches, but there are also settings of 5.9 and 7.1 inches. While drivers can choose the level via a cockpit switch, should they drive away at the top height, the car will automatically settle down to 5.9 at 50 miles per hour and 4.7 at 100 miles per hour . . . and back up again as the car slows. The shock absorbers are also under driver control, either automatically adjusting according to speed or

Here's what causes the drooling: a 2.9-liter version of Porsche's famous flat-six with a pair of KKK sequential turbochargers and 450 horsepower. Climbing through the 959's six gears, you get a second, substantial turbo rush as the tach needle winds past 4,200 rpm.

being set on the soft setting. Features of the 959 also include specific upper and lower A-arm suspensions at both ends, ABS brakes, and a Bosch system that warns of a tire deflating.

While several of these features were common in 2000, they were quite new and impressive on the production 959 in 1986 . . . all part of an imposing system created by Porsche—and a very potent one.

With a 0-to-60 time of 3.9 seconds and a top speed just over 200 miles per hour, the 959 was a flat-out world beater in its day. It proved its worth in the off-road world of the Paris-Dakar rally, where it was a two-time winner, and on the track in the 24 Hours of Le Mans, winning its class and finishing seventh overall in 1986 (as a Porsche 961).

The granddaddy of the recent crops of four-wheel-drive Porsche Turbos, the 959 was a wondercar in its day, though on my drive day I was just wondering when traffic would clear. When it finally did, the gas pedal went to the floor. Whoosh, we whistled up through third gear, the second turbo kicking in dramatically to pick up the pace. Up a gear, hard on the gas, but, oh no, way up ahead cars are beginning to reappear in the fast lanes. The needle creeps up to 280 kilometers per hour . . . 290 . . . 300 . . . just a needle width over the 300—some 185 miles per hour—then back out of the gas.

Rats. But, you can't take a 959 home to Porsche in Zuffenhausen bent or bruised.

PORSCHE 959

Base price: $280,00

Specifications

General

Layout	rear engine, all-wheel drive
Wheelbase (in.)	89.5
Overall length (in.)	167.7
Overall width (in.)	72.4
Overall height (in.)	50.4
Curb weight (lbs.)	3,190

Drivetrain

Engine	twin-turbo dohc 24-valve flat-six
Bore x stroke (mm)	95.0x67.0
Displacement (cc)	2,849
Horsepower	450 bhp @ 6,500 rpm
Torque	370 lb-ft @ 5,500 rpm
Transmission	six-speed manual

Body & Chassis

Front suspension	upper and lower A-arms, coil springs, dual tube shocks, anti-roll bar
Rear suspension	upper and lower A-arms, coil springs, dual tube shocks, anti-roll bar
Steering	rack and pinion, power assist
Brakes	12.7-inch front, 11.9-inch rear, ABS
Wheels	8x17 front, 9x17 rear
Tires	235/45VR-17 front, 255/40VR-17 rear

Performance

0 to 60 mph	3.9 seconds
Top speed	205 mph

When automobile designers talk about a car's "shoulders," this is what they mean. Those substantial fender flares blend out from the original 911 body, as Porsche bases all its special editions—even many of its race cars—on the well-proven 911 body structure.

PORSCHE 911 GT1

For decades, Porsche has been messing around with its famous 911. While keeping the basic rear-engine body shape, it has blown out the fenders like balloons to cover ever-wider tires, fixed all manner of huge wings to the famous shape, altered the engine displacement up and down, and bolted on great turbochargers. It has looked a bit meaner and nastier each year.

From all this fiddling around we got the famous 935 Turbos, the 959, even a version called "Moby Dick." How much farther could Porsche go with the same basic car?

How about the GT1?

Here's what happened. In the mid-1990s, new endurance racing rules for Grand Touring cars set up an interesting proposition. To enter a car in the GT1 series, the automaker

To meet the GT1 racing rules of the mid-1990s, an automaker couldn't race in that category unless it built a road-going version of the car with which it wanted to compete. The company didn't have to build many of the cars, but it had to meet safety and emissions rules, which is why we have this photo of a Porsche GT1 on the road in Germany. *Ulli Upietz*

Okay, it looks a little busy, but this is the cockpit of the full-race Porsche GT1. The *Strasseversion* was more accommodating to driver and passenger, though you would never mistake it for an overstuffed luxury car. *Ulli Upietz*

had to have a street version of that machine. They didn't have to build a lot of that model, but they did need to produce machines that met all the applicable laws—such as emissions regs—that make a car street legal.

The series started out to be a Porsche 911 playground. With its many years of experience and a huge bin of proven speed parts, the Stuttgart company could easily build street-legal versions of the 911 to suit about any racing and government rules in the world. It did, and 911s won that first year.

Then along came the McLaren F1. With its 6.1-liter BMW V-12 and the genius of Gordon Murray behind it, the British car became dominant, even winning the 24 Hours of

Le Mans . . . and sending Porsche engineers back to the drawing boards at the company's Weissach, Germany, engineering center.

What they created was the GT1. First seen in March 1996, the car was built as both a race car and road-going *Strasseversion*. In fact, in a turnabout from the usual way things happen, the street GT1 was developed from the race car.

Both versions retained much of the standard 911 structure from the front back through the passenger compartment, albeit suitably beefed up and stiffened. To the back they bolted a tubular frame that had the classic flat-six engine, but turned around, making this the first mid-engine 911.

Typical of a Porsche factory effort, the GT1 did just what it was designed to do, win the 1998 24 Hours of Le Mans. Even tuned for the street the super Porsche covered the time from 0 to 60 miles per hour in just 3.4 seconds. *Ulli Upietz*

Down over this Porsche seemed to droop one of the most outrageous bodies ever designed for a road-going automobile. It was obviously a 911, but the fender flares of the carbon-fiber bodywork appeared to stretch into the next county. There was a roof-mounted scoop for air to the engine. The flat tail and its tall spoiler were pure race car.

Inside it was also obviously a 911, because the dashboard came straight off the production line. But the car's racing purpose was evident in the typical high-sided driving seats. Inner door panels that looked to be sculptures in carbon fiber added to the racer image.

Fixed behind this passenger compartment was the latest in the long line of variations on the flat-six engine. Racing regs kept the displacement at 3.2 liters, but Porsche was allowed turbos and took full advantage with a pair that work in unison (not sequentially like the 959) to stuff as much as 14.7 psi of charge into the water-cooled six.

For the street GT1, this combination takes the 3.2 to 544 horsepower at 7,000 rpm, with 442 lb-ft of torque at 4,250 rpm. Tuned for racing, the six really howls, with 600 horsepower at 7,200 rpm and 480 lb-ft of torque at 3,950 rpm. That last engine in its most successful racing form was matched to

The "civilian" version of the GT1 had 544 horsepower and 442 lb-ft of torque from the highly pressurized 3.2-liter turbo flat-six. Tuned for racing, the engine screamed up to 600 horsepower and 480 lb-ft of torque. *Ulli Upeitz*

a six-speed sequential gearbox, while the *strasse* machine had a standard Porsche six-speed.

There were other variations from street to race GT1s. While both versions had power-assisted steering, the road machines had steel brake discs while the latter used carbon discs. The cars meant for the vagaries of common roads were given a bit more ride height and a *slightly* softer suspension, but Porsche did not dial the *Strasseversion* a long way back from those meant for such tracks as Le Mans.

With acceleration that could get it to 60 miles per hour in 3.4 seconds, skidpad numbers over 1.0, and the legendary Porsche reliability, the GT1 did precisely what it was designed to do. In 1996, GT1s finished 2-3 at Le Mans, winning their class. And then in 1998, a Porsche GT1 "Evo" not only won the 24 Hours of Le Mans, but was laps and laps ahead of the McLaren F1.

PORSCHE 911 GT1

Base price:	$1,000,000

Specifications
General

Layout	mid-engine, rear drive
Wheelbase (in.)	113.0
Overall length (in.)	185.4
Overall width (in.)	78.0
Overall height (in.)	46.2
Curb weight (lbs.)	2,480

Drivetrain

Engine	twin-turbo dohc 24-valve flat-six
Bore x stroke (mm)	95.0x74.4
Displacement (cc)	3,164
Horsepower	544 bhp @ 7,000 rpm
Torque	442 lb-ft @ 4,250 rpm
Transmission	six-speed manual

Body & Chassis

Front suspension	upper and lower A-arms, coil springs, tube shocks, anti-sway bar
Rear suspension	upper and lower A-arms, coil springs, tube shocks, anti-sway bar
Steering	rack and pinion, power assist
Brakes	15.0-inch vented discs front, 15.9-inch vented discs rear, ABS
Wheels	11x18 front, 13x18 rear
Tires	295/35ZR-18 front, 335/30ZR-18 rear

Performance

0 to 60 mph	3.4 seconds
Top speed	193 mph

MERCEDES-BENZ VISION SLR

For the past decade, Mercedes-Benz has been blending its heritage with modern times and producing some exciting performance cars. The 600SL is high speed with a luxury touch, the E55 sedan a four-door rocket. And now the Vision SLR show car—unveiled at the 1999 Detroit Auto Show—is evidence that the company is ready to soar into the supercar stratosphere. Scheduled to go into production in 2003, the car will cost around $300,000 and only 600 will be made each year.

The SLR's dramatic exterior design is heavily influenced by the 1998 Formula 1 constructors' championship-winning 1998 McLaren-Mercedes. This is particularly true in the nose, which is meant to resemble the front wings of the Grand Prix car.

McLaren's mid-engine F1 car did not influence the SLR's profile, which has the exaggerated long hood/compact cabin/short rear deck proportions seen in treasured prewar performance Mercedes. The SLR's is a very lithe, athletic shape

Mercedes-Benz takes a giant step into the supercar ranks with the Vision SLR, which is expected to cost around $300,000. Front-end styling hints at cues from the championship McLaren-Mercedes Formula 1 cars. For safety reasons, Mercedes opted for Lamborghini-like swing-up doors instead of the gullwing doors of its famous 300SL.

The interior detailing of the Vision SLR includes these oval metal pedals.

And wouldn't this be a wonderful place to spend the day. Mercedes designers continued the Formula 1 theme inside the Vision SLR and then finished the cockpit in aluminum and leather. The slim carbon-fiber seats ride on little shock absorbers to add to driver and passenger comfort.

Engine specialist AMG got the nod to do the SLR's engine. They begin with the 5.5-liter V-8 used in Mercedes' performance cars and top it with a mechanically-driven supercharger and intercooler. Dynamometers put horsepower at 557, with 530 lb-ft of torque for a 0-to-60 time of 4.0 seconds.

that ends in a rather high tail and has an airy greenhouse. The car's drag coefficient is 0.29, and the nose, combined with the high trunk lid, are said to lessen aerodynamic lift at speed.

Mercedes carried the F1 theme up the hood, into the interior and down a prominent center console. The feeling inside is simple, light, and open thanks to the greenhouse and the silver paint and beige suede finish. The seats are two-piece carbon-fiber shells that sit atop spring absorbers for added comfort. Behind each seat is a removable matching suede backpack.

Simplicity was also key to the instrument design, with all readouts fitting in a pair of round gauges ahead of the driver. The majority of functions such as climate control, lights, and the driving mode of the automatic transmission are on four large round switches on the center console. There is also a navigation/TV display and a CD player.

Drivers enter the cockpit via swing-up doors. For safety reasons, Mercedes has replaced the gullwings of the 1950s with doors that are attached to the A-pillar and swing up 75 degrees for entry.

Mercedes chose a combination of aluminum and carbon fiber for the body. There is aluminum in the front and rear sections where it will deform in the case of an accident. The carbon fiber is a major component in the central cabin, providing an extra strong safety capsule. Mercedes figures the use of aluminum and carbon fiber trims weight by 40 percent over a steel structure.

Aluminum is also a major component in the SLR's suspension, which is a four-link design at the front and uses five links at the rear. Naturally, the supercar's suspension will have all the latest gee-whiz technology such as Electronic Stability Program, though this time ESP is also tied into the braking system. In addition to the ABS signals, a computer takes in such data as steering angle and lateral acceleration so it can individually brake each wheel as needed. The electro-hydraulic brakes have fiber-reinforced ceramic discs that weigh 67 percent less and can handle twice the heat of cast-iron brakes.

The wheel-tire combination for the SLR has Bridge-stones, 245/35ZR-19s front and 285/30ZR-20s rear, mounted on aluminum wheels.

The SLR's powerplant is based on Mercedes' 5.5-liter, 24-valve V-8 and is built by AMG, the small specialist firm that Mercedes bought to be its sports department. In hand-building the SLR's V-8s, AMG will add a compact mechanical blower and intercooler between the cylinder banks. AMG expects the V-8 to produce 557 horsepower at 6,500 rpm and 530 lb-ft of torque peaking at 4,000 rpm. The transmission is a five-speed automatic that can be manually shifted via a steering wheel–mounted lever.

Mercedes figures the SLR will get to 60 miles per hour in around 4 seconds and to 125 miles per hour in a tick over 11 seconds on its way up to 200 miles per hour.

While the SLR's design is from Mercedes, the production car will be a joint effort of the automaker and McLaren. Gordon Murray, who designed the McLaren F1, will be the SLR's technical director. The English firm—in which Mercedes has an equity interest—will produce the car in a purpose-built factory. Mercedes' side of the equation is to supply the engine, gearbox, brakes, safety systems, and the structure for front and rear crash protection.

Best of all, there will be variations on the SLR theme beginning with a convertible. Makes you wonder what else they might have up their corporate sleeve.

Previous pages: Like the automaker's Formula 1 team, the SLR combines the talents of Mercedes-Benz and McLaren, the latter's famed engineering genius Gordon Murray acting as technical director. The long-hood, short-deck SLR will be built as both a coupe and convertible.

MERCEDES-BENZ VISION SLR

Base price:	$300,000 (estimated)

Specifications

General

Layout	front engine, rear drive
Wheelbase (in.)	104.7
Overall length (in.)	179.7
Overall width (in.)	73.9
Overall height (in.)	49.1
Curb weight (lbs.)	3,086

Drivetrain

Engine	supercharged dohc 24-valve 5.5-liter V-8
Bore x stroke (mm)	97.0x92.0
Displacement (cc)	5,439
Horsepower	557 bhp @ 6,500 rpm
Torque	530 lb-ft @ 4,000 rpm
Transmission	five-speed automatic

Body & Chassis

Front suspension	na*
Rear suspension	na*
Steering	rack and pinion, power assist
Brakes	electro-hydraulic, fiber-reinforced ceramic discs
Wheels	8.5x19 front, 10x20 rear
Tires	245/35ZR-19 front, 285/30ZR-20 rear

Performance

0 to 60 mph	4.0 seconds (estimated)
Top speed	200 mph (estimated)

*na=not available

chapter 2

ITALY

I f there is a true home of exotic cars, it is Italy. Is it the fine wines and pasta? No, but Italy does have a tradition of engineering excellence, thanks to such companies as Alfa Romeo, Lancia, and Fiat. Many Americans find this difficult to understand because the United States never got or appreciated in their day the fine products of these automakers. Names such as Lancia Lambda or Aurelia; Alfa Romeo P2, P3, or Alfetta; Fiat 805 or Topolino mean little in North America.

Also unappreciated are the engineers behind those great cars. Although Americans know the names of such great automotive leaders as Enzo Ferrari and Ferruccio Lamborghini, few have heard of renowned engineers Vittorio Jano, Dante Giacosa, Carlo Chiti, Gioachino Colombo, Giotto Bizzarrini, Mauro Forghieri, or Aurelio Lampredi . . . to name just a few.

Italy is also home to the world's greatest automotive design houses. While exotic automotive design became much more international during the last decade of the twentieth cen-

tury, up to that point northern Italy—particularly Torino—was its spiritual center. Pininfarina, Bertone, and Italdesign are the modern giants, but the country's history also contains respected names such as Zagato, Vignale, Boano, and Michelotti. Add a wealth of craftsmen and artisans who can weld a chassis, form exquisite aluminum (and now carbon fiber) panels, and cast and machine almost any metal.

Never discount the passion of the Italian people for great automobiles. You can see it publicly in the enthusiasm of the crowds at the Monza or Imola Grand Prix races or along the route of the historic Mille Miglia rally. Those of us who have had the pleasure of driving a Ferrari, Maserati, or Lamborghini on public roads, into huge cities, or through small villages can attest to the depth of this fundamental feeling and excitement for great automobiles in Italy—all of which conspire to make Italy the birthplace of many of the world's most exotic cars.

FERRARI F50

Here's why you might want to consider becoming an automotive journalist: It's late in the day in Maranello, Italy, home to Ferrari. You've been at the automaker's famous Fiorano test track for most of the afternoon with a crew from *Road & Track* testing all the Ferrari models. That part is finished and the photography is wrapped up. And sitting there is the Ferrari F50. The track is still open and we can't have an F50 feeling neglected, can we?

Walk over and open the lightweight carbon-fiber driver's door. Step over the wide sill and drop into red-and-black upholstered seats. Carbon fiber is all around, dashboard, door panels, and center console. Ahead is a small instrument pod with a speedo that cranks up to 360 kilometers per hour—just shy of 225 miles per hour—how daunting . . . rather like the car's $480,000 price tag.

But you solider on, pushing the button that fires up the 513-horsepower 5.0-liter V-12 behind you. According to *R&T*'s computers, that engine will get this 2,710-pound car to 60 miles per hour in 3.6 seconds. Let's try it.

Grabbing the carbon-fiber shift knob, you're into first and with surprisingly light clutch pressure the F50 pulls away. No fuss, no embarrassing two or three tries to match revs and pedal.

With those sticky P335/30ZR-18 Goodyear Eagles, you get well into the throttle, rocketing away from the pits with no fear of wheelspin. The redline is 8,500, but we're shifting at

Despite its exotic nature, the F50 is not a beast to drive, with reasonably light efforts for steering, brakes, and clutch. The Ferrari can be a semi-race car in the right hands, like those of Grand Prix champion, Phil Hill, here giving famous journalist Peter Egan a high-speed ride.

Opposite: Ferrari's F50 was debuted in 1996, the second supercar offering from Maranello, succeeding the famous F40. Compared to the earlier model, Pininfarina softened the exterior styling of the carbon-fiber bodywork for the F50, which was an open roadster with a detachable hardtop.

Having a more civilized cockpit than the F40, the F50 nicely mixes race and road car images in the supercar, with beautifully finished carbon-fiber surfaces. The chassis is based on a central carbon-fiber structure that, like a Formula 1 car, has the suspension attached to it.

8,000, captivated by the howling Ferrari noises behind us. Then onto brakes so powerful it's immediately obvious you're well short of the ultimate braking area.

You quickly come to realize that while an expert like Michael Schumacher can get this thing around Fiorano at lightning speed, it is such a civilized, well-balanced, smoothed-out motorcar that even you can safely get up a good head of steam.

But then, trying to take a Ferrari F50 to the limit is not the point of this drive. It's that glorious sound, the acceleration that flattens you in your seat, the sound of the wind rushing into the cockpit . . . and the idea of driving quickly in a limited-production Ferrari on Fiorano. Wow.

The F50 was, of course, the second small-series supercar from Ferrari. The F40 arrived in the summer of 1987 at a dramatic unveiling in Maranello, which was the last time many of us saw Enzo Ferrari. Delicious pandemonium, the "old man" looking on as the wraps came off the F40, the press going nuts . . .

That one only cost $250,000, with its winged, sharp-edged Pininfarina styling and 478-horsepower turbocharged 3.0-liter V-8. Carbon fiber and Kevlar were used for both the bodywork and as reinforcement for the steel tube frame. The car was a wonderful mix of road and track, race-bred upper and lower A-arm suspensions, and fat tires giving it track manners, but with the option of any of three types of racing or road seats.

For the F50 engine, Ferrari opted for a non-supercharged V-12. With 513 horsepower and 347 lb-ft of torque, the delightfully noisy engine will fire the F50 like a speeding bullet to 60 miles per hour in 3.6 seconds, not pausing until the car is around 202 miles per hour.

Air conditioning was on the option list for the enclosed F40, but you could only get sliding plastic side windows.

Performance testing put the F40's 0-to-60 time at 3.8 seconds, with the top speed around 195 miles per hour. And very quickly the F40 became a worldwide automotive icon.

For 1996, Ferrari came back with the F50, trying to give its customers the feeling of driving a Formula 1 car on the street. Again Pininfarina did the exterior design, but this time the car was sexier, rounder, more liquid.

Like an F1 car, the central carbon-fiber structure had the steering and front suspension connected to it. As in a race car, the V-12, six-speed transaxle, and rear suspension were one unit, the upper and lower A-arm suspensions using pushrods and rockers for spring and shock actuation. The engine was an F1 development, taken out to 4,699 cc and 513 horsepower, yet tuned to meet emissions laws—and all lovingly developed into one of the most exciting road cars of the twentieth century.

The F50 is also a more civilized machine than the F40, not so hard-edged . . . and it even has roll-up windows.

While pushing the F50 to your personal limit around Fiorano, all that fades a bit. What matters are the Ferrari sounds behind you, the power under your right foot, and the joy of being right here, right now, doing just this.

FERRARI F50

Base price:	$480,000

Specifications

General

Layout	mid-engine, rear drive
Wheelbase (in.)	101.6
Overall length (in.)	176.4
Overall width (in.)	78.2
Overall height (in.)	44.1
Curb weight (lbs.)	2,710

Drivetrain

Engine	dohc 60-valve V-12
Bore x stroke (mm)	85.0x69.0
Displacement (cc)	4,699
Horsepower	513 bhp @ 8,500 rpm
Torque	347 lb-ft @ 6,500 rpm
Transmission	six-speed manual

Body & Chassis

Front suspension	upper and lower A-arms, pushrods, rockers, coil springs, tube shocks, anti-roll bar
Rear suspension	upper and lower A-arms, pushrods, rockers, coil springs, tube shocks, anti-roll bar
Steering	rack and pinion, power assist
Brakes	14.0-inch vented discs front, 13.2-inch vented discs rear
Wheels	18x8-1/2 front, 18x13 rear
Tires	P245/35ZR-18 front, P335/30ZR-18 rear

Performance

0 to 60 mph	3.6 seconds
Top speed	202 mph

FERRARI 360 MODENA

Tradition is at the heart and soul of every Ferrari. The famous Italian company has more than 50 years of building strikingly beautiful automobiles and winning race cars . . . and has its sainted founder, Enzo Ferrari. But if you think the renowned Italian automaker is rooted in the past, you are wrong. Executives and engineers in Maranello are well aware that if they let their minds get mired in yesterday and don't advance, Ferrari could quickly become nothing more than a memory.

Their 360 Modena is the evidence of this forward thinking.

For one thing, it doesn't look like the Ferraris of the past. Pininfarina has designed most street Ferraris since the mid-1950s, and you can see its fine, traditional hand in the rear 3/4 view of the car. However, the front of the car has changed. Gone is the classic central eggcrate grille, replaced by a pair of smaller grilles at the ends of the nose.

Why mess with traditional success? Modern aerodynamics. Ferrari engineers put in more than 5,000 wind tunnel hours fine-tuning the shape of the 360 Modena. By dividing

As with most Ferraris in the past 50 years, the 360 Modena was designed by Pininfarina. The tail carries a resemblance to the car's big brother, the 550 Maranello, while the V-8 engine can be viewed through the large rear window. Under the bodywork is an advanced aluminum frame structure.

When Ferrari developed the 3.6-liter V-8 for the 360 Modena, it upped the F355's horsepower by 20 to 395. While torque was increased by only 7 lb-ft, its curve was greatly broadened, offering the maximum 275 lb-ft from 4,750 rpm up to the 7,500 rpm redline.

the grille and coolant radiators into two parts, they created a center inlet channel for air going under the car. This channel, combined with a smooth, sealed underbody and carefully tweaked upper surfaces, not only produces a low drag coefficient of 0.355, but also endows the 360 with natural downforce that increases with speed. The advantage? A car with excellent high-speed stability, but without the need for external spoilers . . . just like the McLaren F1, but at a fraction of its price.

Ferrari turned away from tradition for another crucial part of the 360, the frame. Production cars from Modena have had steel tube frames, but the 360 marks the automaker's conversion to an aluminum inner structure. Developed with Alcoa, the

frame is a lightweight latticework of castings, extrusions, and carefully formed sheet metal covered by aluminum bodywork. Despite being slightly bigger than its predecessor, the F355, the 360 Modena chassis is 28 percent lighter than the 355's and significantly stiffer.

Ferrari kept and refined the F355's upper and lower A-arm suspensions. The brakes are 13-inch vented Brembos with a sophisticated Bosch anti-lock system that can be turned off for high-performance driving.

Ferrari began with the 355's 40-valve V-8, but increased the displacement to 3.6 liters and added refinements. Horsepower went up by a significant 20 to 395 at 8,500 rpm, but the

Pininfarina updated the traditional Ferrari interior for the 360 Modena, mixing leather and aluminum. This version has the steering column–mounted electronic gearshift paddles, the system having separate center console switches for reverse gear and for fully automatic in-town driving. Another switch controls the firmness of the shock absorbers.

truly important difference is torque. Though upped by only 7 lb-ft to 275, that torque is in a dramatically broadened curve. By 4,750 rpm, the V-8 is already at its torque peak and it stays right there up to 7,500 rpm.

Ferrari will match that V-8 with either of two six-speed gearboxes: the traditional manual or the F1-style paddle shifter. The great majority of 360 buyers will opt for the paddle, and it's great fun. From a stop, you pull at the right paddle for first gear, push

down on the throttle and quickly accelerate away. To shift up, a quick paddle flip puts you up a gear. Do the same with the left-hand paddle and it's down one gear. Great fun, and in no time you can pretend to be Michael Schumacher in his Formula 1 car. Ferrari claims the F1 star is as quick around its Fiorano test track with the paddle-shifter 360 as with the manual gearbox.

There is, however, a good argument for the traditional. No one has done production car shift gates as crisp, good-looking,

FERRARI 360 MODENA

Base price: $145,000

Specifications
General

Layout	mid-engine, rear drive
Wheelbase (in.)	102.4
Overall length (in.)	176.3
Overall width (in.)	75.7
Overall height (in.)	47.8
Curb weight (lbs.)	3,065

Drivetrain

Engine	dohc 40-valve V-8
Bore x stroke (mm)	85.0x79.0
Displacement (cc)	3,584
Horsepower	395 bhp @ 8,500 rpm
Torque	275 lb-ft @ 4,750 rpm
Transmission	six-speed manual

Body & Chassis

Front suspension	upper and lower A-arms, coil springs, tube shocks, anti-roll bar
Rear suspension	upper and lower A-arms, coil springs, tube shocks, anti-roll bar
Steering	rack and pinion, variable power assist
Brakes	13.0-inch vented discs front and rear, ABS
Wheels	18x7-1/2 front, 18x9-1/2 rear
Tires	215/45ZR-18 front, 275/40ZR-18 rear

Performance

0 to 60 mph	4.3 seconds
Top speed	189 mph (estimated)

For the 360 Modena's front end, Pininfarina turned away from the traditional Ferrari single eggcrate front grille for a pair of smaller side grilles. The area between the grilles is the inlet area for the under-car aerodynamics, which produce excellent high-speed stability without external spoilers.

and easy to use as Ferrari's. Going up or down a gear, there's a wonderful metallic snap—a sound of confirmation—to each cog change.

Regardless of the gearbox, the 360 Modena is a car with two natures. The torquey V-8 is amazingly flexible, allowing effortless around-town driving even with the revs under 1,000 rpm. The car's nicely laid-out cabin is roomy and extremely comfortable, with a stirring sound system and an air conditioning system that will cool you on the most dreadfully hot summer days in Italy. Put the shock absorber ride control switch on soft and just trundle around town like any sport coupe.

Or head out of town, flip the shock switch back to firm, turn off the stereo, and hammer down the throttle. This is what a Ferrari is meant to do, turning in easily in tight turns, ready to be balanced on the throttle before blasting down the next straight, the brakes hauling you down safely corner after corner.

Creating a Ferrari that can drive down a twisting road about as fast as any car in the world is one bit of tradition the company won't change.

FERRARI 550 MARANELLO

Front-engine Ferrari Grand Touring cars have been an important part of the Italian automaker's history since its first days in the late 1940s. Four of Ferrari's victories in the rugged Mille Miglia open road race came in closed-coupe Ferraris powered by V-12s. Generations of great Ferrari GTs followed, adding such famous names as Tour de France, SWB, GTO, and GTB to the company's honor roll.

But then the lineage faded. In the early 1970s, the exotic-car world went mid-engine and Ferrari was with them. To counter Lamborghini's Countach, Maranello created the 1973 365 GTB/4 Berlinetta Boxer with its flat-12 behind the passenger cockpit. This was Maranello's top-line production GT, replaced in 1984 by the Testarossa, a mid-engine line that continued until 1997. Along the way, Ferrari developed its

There's almost a sly smile on the eggcrate grille of Ferrari's 550 Maranello. In addition to giving a classic Ferrari face to the two-seat Grand Touring car, the front end is part of an overall aerodynamics package on the car that includes a clean, flat bottom and short-spoiler tail.

What's inside a $250,000 Grand Touring car? Comfortable, supportive leather-upholstered seats. An instrument and controls layout that is a prototype for how it should be done. A shifter for the six-speed gearbox that is set in a beautifully hewn metal gate.

"smaller" mid-engine V-8 sports car, starting with the 308 in 1975 and continuing today with the 360 Modena. There were also ultra exotic Ferrari mid-engine supercars, the 1987 F40 and 1996 F50.

Impressive as the Testarossa looked and performed, it was a bit of a truck to drive in traffic. Like the Lamborghini Diablo, it was quite wide, more so in the back than the front, making it a bear to maneuver in anything but wide-open spaces. So when it came time to replace the aging "TR" in the mid-1990s, Ferrari went back to its Grand Touring roots and developed an all-new front-engine supercar, the 550 Maranello.

As expected, long-time Ferrari partner, Pininfarina, did the bodywork, which seems to integrate the classic Ferrari

grille in flaring nostrils . . . aggressive without being pushy. With the front-engine layout we again get the classic long hood/short deck proportions, And, by the way, a good aerodynamic package, thanks to the 550's flat bottom and blunt, spoilered tail.

Inside is generous seating for two in a leather-lined cockpit with the wonderful aroma of one of those famous Italian leather shops. The design is a classic: no-nonsense white-on-black gauges in a driver-oriented layout that puts everything from the tall shifter to air conditioning controls just a short reach away.

For the 550 Maranello, Ferrari returned to the traditional V-12, but with the most up-to-date electronics. The model's designation, 550, stands for the displacement of the engine,

Under the Pininfarina bodywork of the 550 Maranello is a chassis with upper and lower A-arms at the front and wide-based H-arms for the rear suspension. Other chassis features include electronically adjustable shock absorbers, huge disc brakes, and variable-assist rack-and-pinion steering.

which is 5,474 cc. With dual camshafts per head and four valves per cylinder, the all-aluminum V-12 puts out 485 horsepower at 7,000 rpm and 419 lb-ft of torque at 5,000 rpm.

Impressive as those numbers are, they don't tell the whole story. More than just powerful, with a 0-to-60 time of 4.7 seconds, the Maranello V-12 is amazingly flexible throughout the power ranges.

What are the tricks? How about advanced electronic engine management? Or computer-controlled variable-length runners in the intake manifold? Or an exhaust system that lessens backpressure as speed rises?

The chassis engineers were just as busy. They started with upper and lower A-arms for the front suspension, using wider-based H-arms at the back. Supplementing the coil springs and anti-sway bars are electronically adjustable shock absorbers. Matched with a 50/50 weight balance, monster disc brakes, and variable-assist rack-and-pinion steering, the Maranello becomes, well, a car for all scenes and seasons.

There was a time when a high-performance car of this sort would have been a single-nature weekend car. Rough riding. Fussy engine. Few creature comforts.

FERRARI 550 MARANELLO

Base price: $204,000

Specifications

General

Layout	front engine, rear drive
Wheelbase (in.)	98.4
Overall length (in.)	179.1
Overall width (in.)	76.2
Overall height (in.)	50.3
Curb weight (lbs.)	3,725

Drivetrain

Engine	dohc 48-valve V-12
Bore x stroke (mm)	88.0x75.0
Displacement (cc)	5,474
Horsepower	485 bhp @ 7,000 rpm
Torque	419 lb-ft @ 5,000 rpm
Transmission	six-speed manual

Body & Chassis

Front suspension	upper and lower A-arms, coil springs, tube shocks, anti-roll bar
Rear suspension	upper and lower H-arms, coil springs, tube shocks, anti-roll bar
Steering	rack and pinion, variable power assist
Brakes	13.0-inch vented discs front, 12.2-inch vented discs rear, ABS
Wheels	18x8-1/2 front, 18x10-1/2 rear
Tires	255/40ZR-18 front, 295/35ZR-18 rear

Performance

0 to 60 mph	4.7 seconds
Top speed	199 mph (estimated)

The 550 in the Ferrari's name refers to the engine's displacement, which is 5,474 cc. Power from the all-aluminum V-12 is 485 horsepower and 419 lb-ft of torque, enough to get the 3,725-pound supercar to 60 miles per hour in just 4.7 seconds, and to almost 200 miles per hour.

Not anymore. With the electronic shocks comes a dual-nature chassis, soft enough on its city setting to soak up ordinary road imperfections and divots. Set it on firm, however, and you have a near-race car that corners flat with a neutral attitude that can be tuned with the throttle.

Spin it to the 7,700-rpm redline in any gear, where it makes a wonderful loud and slightly rowdy Ferrari roar. Or slap it into fourth gear at under 1,000 rpm and feel it pull strongly away without protest. You can work the six-speed manual gearbox for every mile per hour or use second or third gear for most all your in-city driving.

And what amenities do you require? A concert-hall sound system? Heating and air conditioning that are as effective as any car's in the world? The 550 obliges.

Best yet, if you have any special requirements, from a favorite color to carbon-fiber seats to a sturdy roll bar, Ferrari will custom build your 550 Maranello.

BUGATTI EB110

To many historians, Ettore Bugatti is one of the half-dozen most venerated men in automotive history. The Italian-born, Alsace-based intuitive engineer is right up there with Henry Ford, Enzo Ferrari, Colin Chapman, Gottlieb Daimler, and Dr. Ferdinand Porsche. All were strong-willed men who created exactly the automobiles they felt the world should have—no compromises—and the results are honored in auto museums around the world.

Bugatti's Type 35 is considered a landmark race car. Some Type 57s are thought to have among the most seductive bodywork ever fixed to an automotive chassis. Bugatti Royales are among the largest, rarest, and most expensive automobiles ever made. And while Bugatti's creations varied from two-seater race cars to the massive Royales, the thing that distinguished them all was a marvelous balance of the science and the art of engineering.

The renowned Bugatti name was revived in the late 1980s with the development of this very exotic mid-engine supercar. Called the EB110, it was to carry on the great line of automobiles created by legendary engineer Ettore Bugatti. The EB110's design was by Marcello Gandini, who did the Lamborghini Countach and Diablo.

So, it was with a great deal of enthusiasm that we all greeted the news in the late 1980s that Bugatti would be revived in the form of an exotic car to match the likes of Ferrari and Lamborghini.

Italian industrialist Romano Artioli was the man behind the ambitious project, though the true source of money was a mystery, which added to the exotic nature of the endeavor. The unveiling of the EB110 in Paris in 1991 was a grand affair of royal proportions that just reeked of big money.

The EB110 seemed worthy of the fuss, a new star in its French blue finish. Marcello Gandini, who gets design credit for the Lamborghini Countach and Diablo, drew the shape of the EB110. The car has an undeniable presence, a miniature of the classic Bugatti horseshoe-shaped grille, and tricks such as a rear spoiler that rises when you get underway to add downforce and expose the engine's intercoolers.

The interior could be a tight fit for taller drivers, but what a nice place to be, all finely stitched leather and polished

In keeping with the spectacular approach to the Bugatti project, the car was unveiled at Le Defense in Paris, followed by a black-tie ball at the Palais de Versailles. Bugattis were assembled in a beautiful purpose-built factory near Modena, Italy, the city that is also home to Ferrari, Lamborghini, and Maserati.

Get in an EB110, and you are surrounded by top-quality leather with polished wood trim. The chassis of the Bugatti is made of carbon fiber, the suspensions have upper and lower A-arms, and the fronts use race car–like pushrod actuation.

wood. You nestle into the seats, the tall center console on your right, with gauges ahead of you and switches to your left, your right, and even on the ceiling.

An advanced carbon-fiber chassis provides excellent stiffness for the suspension and drivetrain. Upper and lower A-arm suspensions are used fore and aft, the fronts with race car–like pullrod actuation of the shocks and coil springs.

As in all Bugattis, the true gem is the engine. The 3.5-liter V-12 has five valves per cylinder (three intake, two exhaust) opened by two camshafts in each cylinder head. Fed by fuel injection and pumped up with a pair of IHI turbochargers to 15.2 psi of boost, the Bugatti achieves 611 horsepower at 8,250 rpm.

With torque measuring 480 lb-ft at 4,200 rpm, Bugatti engineers rightfully specified four-wheel drive and hefty Michelins measuring 245/40ZR-18 front and 325/30ZR-18 rear to get all that power to the pavement.

Launching a car with four-wheel drive isn't easy—even an exotic machine with 611 horsepower—but *Road & Track* got an EB110 from 0 to 60 miles per hour in 4.4 seconds. Drive to all wheels really pays in handling tests, as the Bugatti got through the slalom run at 64.3 miles per hour (a McLaren F1 did 64.5 miles per hour) and set the magazine's then-current record on the skidpad, generating 0.99g of lateral acceleration.

In subjective terms, the Bugatti turned out to be a very civilized-handing car with no evil habits and a surprisingly smooth ride.

The EB110 proved to have what everyone expected in an exotic car, from stunning performance to proud beauty to a price tag (had the car ever been sold in the United States) of $350,000. There was even an impressive new factory for the car in Campogalliano, Italy, just outside the country's exotic car capital, Modena.

BUGATTI EB110

Base price: $350,000

Specifications

General

Layout	mid-engine, four-wheel drive
Wheelbase (in.)	100.4
Overall length (in.)	173.2
Overall width (in.)	76.4
Overall height (in.)	43.9
Curb weight (lbs.)	3,940

Drivetrain

Engine	quad-turbo dohc 60-valve V-12
Bore x stroke (mm)	81.0x56.6
Displacement (cc)	3,500
Horsepower	611 bhp @ 8,250 rpm
Torque	480 lb-ft @ 4,200 rpm
Transmission	six-speed manual

Body & Chassis

Front suspension	upper and lower A-arms, coil springs, tube shocks, anti-roll bar
Rear suspension	upper and lower A-arms, dual coil springs, tube shocks, anti-roll bar
Steering	rack and pinion, power assist
Brakes	13.1-inch vented discs front and rear, ABS
Wheels	18x18 front, 18x24 rear
Tires	245/40ZR-18 front, 325/30ZR-18 rear

Performance

0 to 60 mph	4.4 seconds
Top speed	207 mph

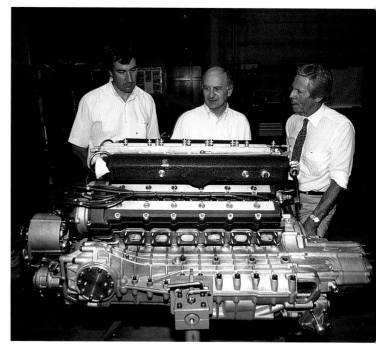

As in all Bugattis, the EB110 engine is quite special, a 60-valve 3.5-liter V-12 sporting an IHI turbocharger for each bank. With 15.2 psi of boost, the engine creates 611 horsepower. Seen with the engine are Michel Bugatti (left), engine designer Paolo Stanzani (center), and famous motoring journalist, Paul Frere.

Sadly, timing and economic conditions didn't cooperate. The exotic-car market stalled and the source of the project's money—whatever it was—dried up. EB110 production was halted and Bugatti went on the block.

Happily, Bugatti did not die. In 1998, Volkswagen bought the bankrupt organization and revived it. The guiding hand behind the purchase? Another brilliant engineer, Ferdinand Piech, chairman of VW-Audi, the grandson of Ferdinand Porsche, and the inspiration behind the Porsche 917. At major auto shows, both VW's design studio and Giorgetto Giugiaro's famed Italdesign began to show new examples of what a new Bugatti could be, either as a hyperexpensive coupe or mid-engine sports car.

The line continues, thanks to VW.

LAMBORGHINI COUNTACH

There has always been something magical about Lamborghini's Countach. Pure enthusiasts gravitate to Ferraris, claiming Maranello's automobiles are better. They may be correct on some levels, but for much of the world's populace what matters most about exotic cars is how they stir your soul . . . and few cars have done it better than the Countach.

Lamborghini beat Ferrari to the mid-12-cylinder-engine market with the Miura in 1966. Another landmark Bertone design, the Miura had begun to age by the end of the decade. Ferruccio Lamborghini went back to Bertone for a new auto-

mobile shape. Unveiled at the Geneva Auto Show in March 1971, the Countach LP500 grabbed all the headlines.

As it turned out, Maranello's experts were at work on a mid-engine supercar and would debut the 365GT Berlinetta Boxer in 1973, beating the Countach to production by a year. But while the famous Boxer has faded a bit into history, the Countach has not.

Bertone's Marcello Gandini gets credit for the Countach's exterior design. Gandini has any number of significant designs to his credit, including the Lancia Stratos and Alfa

Marcello Gandini explained that when designing the Lamborghini Countach, he wanted "people to be astonished when they saw the car." He succeeded, creating possibly THE most recognizable car in the world. While early models were quite clean and pure, later versions grew spoilers and other add-ons.

Romeo Carabo show car, but the Countach is his jewel. He once said he wanted "people to be astonished when they saw the car." He succeeded.

The Countach began as a pure and simple shape. As years passed, the Countach's aluminum body was altered with air scoops, spoilers, and fender flares. Some fans argue that the additions brought an impressive muscular aggressiveness . . . others figure the original shape was best.

Just as Bertone broke new ground with the Countach's exterior, Lamborghini was innovative with the drivetrain. While the Miura's V-12 is mounted transversely (side-to-side), the Countach's is in the more conventional fore-aft location . . . but with a difference.

Instead of positioning the V-12 and gearbox in the expected way—engine behind the passenger compartment, the transmission behind that—they turned the drivetrain around. The five-speed manual gearbox juts into the passenger compartment. The power goes rearward from the transmission via a shaft that passes through the engine sump to the final drive differential. With this layout, the shifter could be mounted directly to the gearbox instead of needing a long complicated linkage from the cockpit around to the back of the V-12.

In its original Countach form, the 4.0-liter V-12 had 375 horsepower, but that was eventually bumped up to 5.2 liters, 455 horsepower at 7,000 rpm, and 368 lb-ft of torque at 5,000 rpm.

This is the view many competitors get of the Countach, going away and accelerating. Debuted at the 1971 Geneva Auto Show, the Countach replaced the groundbreaking Lamborghini Miura, the first serious mid-engine 12-cylinder exotic car. In that era, many automakers, such as Ferrari, Ford, and Porsche, were developing mid-engine designs.

With its engine turned around 90 degrees, the Countach's transmission extends forward into the cockpit, creating a large center console. This widely divides the interior for passenger and driver, the latter facing a classic-looking instrument pod . . . and having the most fun.

Other technical specs include unequal-length upper and lower A-arm suspensions front and rear, with a pair of coil springs and tube shocks per side at the back. Big disc brakes hide inside the Countach's unique alloy wheels.

You pull the Countach's unique doors up to get in, stepping across a wide sill and settling down into the seats. Exotic car seats are often described as form fitting, like a leather-gloved hand. Not this Lambo's, which reminds one more of a chaise lounge from the 1960s. Side support is that wide sill and the tall center console to the right.

You sit low in the Countach, the requisite black-on-white gauges splayed in front. Pull down the door and with a key twist, the car is ready.

Forward into first gear with a metallic thunk and after reasonably light clutch pressure you're away . . . fast. Depending on which form of the Countach you're driving, 60 miles per hour comes up in 4.5 to 5.0 seconds with that unusual big sound of Lamborghini's V-12.

In no time you're whistling along in this wonderful exotic car, putting down the miles and prompting other drivers' smiles.

You must remember two things: One is that you can't see much out of the Countach, and in tight places, it's best to remember how much real estate you're wheeling along. Second, rearward vision is terrible. You need help to back up . . . unless you're as flexible as Lamborghini's factory test drivers. Men such as the famous Valentino Balboni back up a

LAMBORGHINI COUNTACH

Base price: $145,000

Specifications
General
Layout	mid-engine, rear drive
Wheelbase (in.)	96.5
Overall length (in.)	168.0
Overall width (in.)	78.7
Overall height (in.)	42.1
Curb weight (lbs.)	3,263

Drivetrain
Engine	dohc 24-valve V-12
Bore x stroke (mm)	85.5x69.0
Displacement (cc)	4,754
Horsepower	375 bhp @ 7,000 rpm
Torque	303 lb-ft @ 4,500 rpm
Transmission	five-speed manual

Body & Chassis
Front suspension	upper and lower A-arms, coil springs, tube shocks, anti-roll bar
Rear suspension	upper lateral link and reversed lower A-arms, upper and lower trailing arms, dual coil springs, dual tube shocks, anti-roll bar
Steering	rack and pinion
Brakes	11.8-inch vented discs front, 11.2-inch discs rear
Wheels	7.5x15 front, 12x15 rear
Tires	225/50VR-15 front, 345/35VR-15 rear

Performance
0 to 60 mph	4.9 seconds
Top speed	183 mph

While its predecessor, the famous Miura, had a transverse engine, the V-12 in the Countach is located "north-south," with its nose to the back of the car. Early Countachs had a 4.0-liter engine, but this was later increased to 5.2 liters and a very healthy 455 horsepower.

Countach (or, now, a Diablo) while sitting on the wide doorsills looking back over the car; it's more impressive than watching him snake a Countach through tight esses.

However, it is also enjoyable to sit next to Balboni as he pops over the rise at speed on the road to Modena. Just ahead is the famous tight left-hander that has terrified so many customers during test drives, many assuming the car would be catapulted into the field beyond. But the Countach goes slightly nose down as Balboni dabs the brakes at the last moment, slides easily through the corner, and nails the throttle. You take a deep breath and Balboni just grins.

LAMBORGHINI DIABLO VT

It was foggy near Modena, Italy, when they wheeled the all-new Lamborghini Diablo out of the shed for our morning photo session. It was early 1990, and we'd waited almost two decades for the oft-promised-never-delivered successor to the Countach.

It was worth the wait.

Marcello Gandini, who penned the Countach, gets credit for the Diablo's exterior design, though we hear the shape was fine-tuned at Chrysler in Detroit. The interior was all-American,

designed by Bill Dayton while working at Lamborghini in Italy.

Both the exterior and interior beautifully drew on the proportions and design theme of the Countach and updated them . . . softer and more sensuous. While such pieces as the deck lid, engine cover, and sidesills of the Diablo were done in carbon fiber, the main body was aluminum. It fit over a new frame that had square tubes in place of the round tubes used with the Countach. And it was a bit bigger, with the wheelbase

When Lamborghini went to carbon-fiber exterior panels for its Diablo, it also did a minor redesign, including a new lower front chin for the supercar. The parts not done in the lightweight material are the aluminum doors and the steel roof, the latter being part of the car's structure.

Diablo interiors come in several trims; this one is a special version done for the 40th anniversary of the company. All have a broad center console for the gearbox and seats you wiggle over and into before settling down for what should be a great drive.

stretching from 96.5 to 104.3 inches, and overall length growing 10.2 inches to 175.6. The chassis kept the classic upper and lower A-arm suspension layouts.

Like the Countach, the Diablo had the "backward" drivetrain. The "front" of the V-12—now at 5.7 liters and 485 horsepower—was at the very back of the car, the transmission poking forward into the cockpit. This unusual layout proved helpful when Lamborghini developed its VT four-wheel-drive system, which features a viscous coupling and a short

carbon-fiber driveshaft to a front-axle differential. Introduced a few years after the original Diablo, the traction-enhancing four-wheel drive would direct power to the front wheels if the rears ever began to spin more than the fronts.

The Diablo debuted to great excitement and reviews, but its parent company, Chrysler, later sold the small Italian firm, which fell into difficult times. A rebirth came in 1998 when Lamborghini went to Audi, asking to use its V-8 in a new small model. The German company declined, but turned around and

Front-hinged, flip-up doors have been a feature of Lamborghinis since the Countach was debuted. They make getting in and out easier, particularly in tight parking places. This purple Diablo was one of a limited series built to celebrate the automaker's 40th anniversary.

bought Lamborghini. And now, 10 years after photographing the first Diablo, we were back in Italy to do the latest Diablo.

There are mild styling changes, particularly to the nose, but what matters most is that much of the car's bodywork is now tough, lightweight carbon fiber. The only major exceptions are the aluminum doors and the steel roof, the latter a part of the chassis structure.

Carbon fiber shows up in the revised Diablo interior, where it is used extensively on the center console and a new arced dashboard, blending nicely with the leather and aluminum also used inside.

The basics of the suspension didn't change, but the front and rear tracks are a bit wider. The electronically controlled shock absorbers have been improved, and the entire chassis can be better utilized because the Diablo is now stiffer.

The V-12 is opened out to 6.0 liters with horsepower upped to 550 at 7,100 rpm and the torque to 435 lb-ft at 5,500 rpm. The marvelous four-wheel-drive VT system helps spread the power around to all wheels. Get the VT launched properly—rev to 6,000 rpm and side-step the clutch pedal—and the new Diablo smokes its way to 60 miles per hour in just 3.6 seconds. Top speed? Just over 200 miles per hour.

LAMBORGHINI DIABLO VT

Base price: $230,000

Specifications
General

Layout	mid-engine, rear drive or four-wheel drive (VT)
Wheelbase (in.)	104.3
Overall length (in.)	175.6
Overall width (in.)	80.3
Overall height (in.)	43.9
Curb weight (lbs.)	3,865

Drivetrain

Engine	dohc 48-valve V-12
Bore x stroke (mm)	87.0x84.0
Displacement (cc)	5,992
Horsepower	550 bhp @ 7,100 rpm
Torque	435 lb-ft @ 5,500 rpm
Transmission	five-speed manual

Body & Chassis

Front suspension	upper and lower A-arms, coil springs, tube shocks, electronically controlled shocks, anti-roll bar
Rear suspension	upper and lower A-arms, coil springs, tube shocks, electronically controlled shocks, anti-roll bar
Steering	rack and pinion, power assist
Brakes	14.1-inch vented discs front, 13.2-inch vented discs rear, ABS
Wheels	18x8-1/2 front, 18x13 rear
Tires	235/35ZR-18 front, 335/30ZR-18 rear

Performance

0 to 60 mph	3.6 seconds
Top speed	205 mph (estimated)

Diablo V-12s come with either 5.7- or 6.0-liter engines, ranging from 485 horsepower to 550. The engine sits "backward" in the chassis, its transmission jutting forward into the cockpit. The easiest way to get all that power to the ground is the VT four-wheel-drive system.

And all this from a car that's quite civilized. Nuzzle into the clamshell seats and pull down the door. Turn off the combination satellite navigation/television receiver screen so you can concentrate. Reset the electronic shocks from the soft street ride to firm track setting. Get the 6.0 liters burbling behind you. Then onto the circuit.

Not knowing the track layout, we tuck in behind someone who has done it many times and just hang on. Thanks to a broad torque band, there's plenty of power in each of the six gears. Turn-in is ever-so-smooth, and with the four-wheel drive you feel a heightened sense of balance, neither end of the car wanting to dominate. Very quickly you get used to driving the Diablo VT aggressively . . . until you remember this is someone else's $230,000 car.

For all its improvements, the Diablo retains one difficult feature: like the Countach, you can't see out the back. But as my friends at *Road & Track* say, when you drive a Diablo you figure, "What's behind me is not important."

PAGANI ZONDA C12

From the outside there's nothing remarkable about the place. It's another building in still another industrial park, though this one is in Italy's Castelfranco Emilia, a small town just east of Modena. It's no more than a 15-minute drive each to Ferrari, Lamborghini, or Maserati.

This building belongs to Horace Pagani's Modena Design, which has done work for many of the exotic car manufacturers in this fabled automotive Eden, mainly designing and fabricating carbon-fiber components. Upstairs, a studio mixes traditional huge design boards with computers in which body and chassis components can be twirled and tested on-screen. Down in the main shop are huge work areas, including one for laying up carbon fiber, while in another are huge autoclaves for baking the lightweight pieces.

Horace Pagani's dream on wheels, the Zonda C12. Born in Argentina, Pagani moved to Italy to fulfill his dream of creating and building a supercar of his own design. The bodywork is made of carbon fiber in Pagani's own shops, and weighs just 136 pounds.

Detailing, detailing, detailing is the best way to describe the Zonda's interior. Pagani didn't miss designing something into every corner or square inch of the interior—rounded pedals included—and the mixture of leather, aluminum, and carbon fiber gives the car a very contemporary look.

But the most important room in the building is the lobby, because for the moment it contains a Pagani Zonda C12, the car Horace Pagani just had to build.

And here's the remarkable thing: Pagani personally designed the C12's exterior, interior, tub, chassis, and suspension. What's more, he did it the old-fashioned way, by hand on drawing boards before turning the sketches and plans over to his engineers to confirm the design standards in their computers.

In his shops, craftsmen create the Zonda's carbon-fiber tub and exterior body panels, the latter weighing just 136 pounds, 48 of them being the huge rear engine cover. The shape has a jet fighter canopy floating in a race-car lower body inspired by the

Sauber-Mercedes Group C Silver Arrows. The front styling is somewhat predictable, but the rear is a photographer's delight of detailing. The Zonda's aerodynamics have been tested in Dallara's wind tunnel, with a claimed downforce of 285 pounds in front and 330 in back at 125 miles per hour.

Chrome-moly subframes are bolted to the front and rear of the carbon-fiber tub to carry the upper and lower A-arm suspensions and, at the back, the drivetrain. The frames also provide controlled crush for crash tests. Mercedes-Benz supplies the 394-horsepower 6.0-liter or AMG 500-horsepower 7.0-liter V-12, plus electronics, while the gearbox is a ZF six-speed manual.

The reminder of a C12's bought-out components are of equivalent high quality: AP clutch, Brembo ventilated disc brakes, Michelin Pilot tires (255/40ZR-18s front, 345/35ZR-18s back) on OZ wheels, Bilstein shocks, and TRW power rack-and-pinion steering.

While the remarkable detail of the work is obvious in the chassis, it's best seen in the interior, in the leatherwork on the carbon-fiber shell seats, the aluminum instrument pod, and the round brake and clutch pedals. The carbon-fiber surfaces are finished with the care once reserved for the wood in English luxury automobiles.

Whether fitted with the 394- or 500-horsepower V-12, the C12 is a rocket as that horsepower need only accelerate 2,750 pounds. Customers can choose their car's colors and visit the factory for a fitting of what Pagani hopes will be 25 highly personalized cars per year, left- or right-hand drive as you wish. Price? Start at $350,000.

So what is Horace Pagani trying to prove? As a kid, he littered the pages of his school notebooks with automotive designs in his hometown of Casilda (Santa Fe), Argentina. After industrial design studies, he understood he had to go to Italy to realize his automotive dreams. So in 1983, the 27-year-old

Pagani's Zonda C12 design was inspired by Mercedes-Benz's Group C Silver Arrow race cars, with a cockpit meant to mimic that of a fighter aircraft. Using the 550-horsepower V-12, the C12 will rocket to 60 miles per hour in 3.6 seconds on its way to around 190 miles per hour. Price? Around $350,000.

PAGANI ZONDA C12 AND C12 S

Base price: $350,000

Specifications
General

Layout	mid-engine, rear drive
Wheelbase (in.)	107.5
Overall length (in.)	171.1
Overall width (in.)	80.9
Overall height (in.)	45.3
Curb weight (lbs.)	2,750

Drivetrain

Engine	dohc 48-valve V-12
Bore x stroke (mm)	89.0x80.2 (5,987 cc)
Displacement (cc)	5,987 or 7,010
Horsepower	394 bhp @ 5,200 rpm (C12) or 500 bhp @ 5,500 rpm (C12 S)
Torque	410 lb-ft @ 3,800 rpm (C12) or 540 lb-ft @ 4,100 rpm (C12 S)
Transmission	six-speed manual

Body & Chassis

Front suspension	upper and lower A-arms, coil springs, tube shocks, anti-roll bar
Rear suspension	upper and lower A-arms, coil springs, tube shocks, anti-roll bar
Steering	rack and pinion, power assist
Brakes	14.0-inch vented discs front, 13.1-inch vented discs rear
Wheels	na*
Tires	255/40ZR-18 front, 345/35ZR-18 rear

Performance

0 to 60 mph	3.6 seconds (with 550-bhp V-12)
Top speed	190 mph (estimated)

*na=not available

Mercedes-Benz was chosen as the engine supplier, and Pagani offers a choice of two V-12s from the German automaker. The "base" is Mercedes' 394-horsepower 6.0-liter V-12, while the step up is the 7.0-liter AMG edition, hot rodded to 550 horsepower. Both engines come with a six-speed transmission.

Lamborghini fan moved to the Modena area to get a job with that automaker. Already trained in fiberglass methods, Pagani quickly realized that carbon fiber was the future and learned to work with the then-new techniques.

Pagani left Lamborghini in the mid-1980s, but turned his carbon-fiber expertise into a business that has done work for everything from Modena's exotic car makers to major governments.

With the success of these programs came the time, expertise, and funds to begin the sports car. Pagani began work on the car in 1992 and unveiled it at the 1999 Geneva Auto Show, fully certified for low emissions, successfully past its difficult crash test, and with tens of thousands of miles of durability tests already completed—ready for sale.

Is Pagani the next Ferrari or Lamborghini? We'll know in another 10 years, but in the meantime, his car remains a remarkable one-man design feat in a world that sometimes seems overcrowded with design teams.

chapter 3

JAPAN

Wild-looking, hairy chested, high-speed exotic cars do not come naturally to the Japanese. Part of the reason is societal and some of it economic . . . along with a lack of great roads in Japan where you can readily open up a very fast, powerful automobile.

There have been attempts, however. In the early 1990s, Nissan came very close to making a true exotic, a slick-looking all-wheel-drive sports car called the Mid-4 that got well into development before the project was killed. It says a lot about Japanese automakers that Nissan preferred to build the Skyline GTR, a wonderfully nasty-looking four-passenger coupe based on a high-volume model, but modified with twin turbos, all-wheel drive, and the ability to shame many sports cars on a road course.

Individuals have also tried. As an example, for many years the very attractive Made in Japan Gigliato Aerosa was shown at the world's great auto shows. A true exotic with the sophisticated Yamaha-Ford SHO V-8 driveline tucked in behind the driver, the Aerosa never went into production.

Japanese automakers have been willing to build such exotics as the Nissan R390 because they can use them to sell more small cars, but they've never had the courage to put those supercars into serious production. Toyota MR2s and Spyders, Honda S2000s, and years of great Nissan Z-Cars got the nod for the showrooms, but that's the limit.

The Japanese, however, have made a very important contribution to the world of exotic cars, thanks to Honda. Before the debut of the NSX, exotic cars were quick and beautiful, but not very civilized . . . hot in the summer, burdened by questionable cooling systems, and so on . . . weekend cars that might leave you stranded.

Honda, with its exacting engineering and production standards, could never build such a car. So the NSX was not only fast and good looking, but as reliable and comfortable to use as any Accord sedan. Within a generation, other exotic cars had been, for the most part, "NSX-ized."

It's easily arguable that change was a far greater contribution to the exotic car world than still more horsepower and another swoopy-looking body style.

ACURA NSX-T

Acura's NSX is the thinking man's exotic car. While rare, high-performance two-seaters pluck away at our heartstrings, the Honda-designed and -built NSX also appeals to your head and, in a way, to your sense of reason.

This is good news and bad. Good because the NSX need not be just the plaything other exotic cars tend to become. For all their emotional appeal, most of these expensive toys turn into weekend wonders. It could be for any of several reasons, from limited interior space to a fussy drivetrain to the fact the car is—like the Lamborghini Diablo—almost impossible to back up without external assistance.

Not the NSX. For while Honda may lack the interest to create a supercar that makes you truly weak at the knees—and that's the bad side of the news—they are equally incapable of *not* building a well-thought-out, sensible automobile. And in doing so, they changed the exotic car world.

Acura's NSX is the automobile that made other exotic carmakers clean up their act. No more excuses. Before the mid-engine Japanese whiz kid came along, companies could get away with creating a high-priced machine with sizzling good looks and tire-shredding horsepower, but they didn't get all the details quite right: marginal air conditioning, too-heavy

Aluminum is used for much of the NSX, from the body to major pieces in the independent A-arm suspensions. Honda used the exotic car as a development ground to learn more about working with this lightweight material.

Opposite: **The most important Acura NSX was the first version, which set a new standard of quality in the exotic car world. Ferrari's 348 (seen here with the NSX) was not up to the Honda-made sports car's level and sent the Italian engineers to work, dramatically raising the quality of their automobiles.**

pedal pressures, and luggage compartments that would melt lead in the summer.

All that ended with the NSX. Here was a car that came close to the other exotics in all the important areas, from acceleration to handling to a sleek body shape. Given Honda's racing record, it also had a proud competition heritage, which is more than Lamborghini could claim. And yet the NSX was also built to Honda's exacting quality standards, with a cool cabin in the summer, engine noise that entertains the driver without being obtrusive, and a paint finish with no drips.

When Ferrari's first true post-NSX model, the F355, debuted, it had been "Hondaized" into a true two-nature car, both quick and civil. It could be argued that Ferrari did it better. The Italians learned the best parts of the Honda lesson, but kept the Ferrari edge in its cars. Honda, which had dramatically raised the exotic car standards with the NSX, never made the next step forward. By the time Ferrari had moved on one more model to the 360 Modena, Honda still had the NSX . . . by then almost 10 years old.

In all fairness, Ferrari was again copying Honda. By developing the 360 Modena's unit body in aluminum, the Italians were doing something the Japanese had done years before. Add the doors and deck lids, and the Honda's aluminum unit body tips the scale at only 462 pounds. Aluminum is also used for major components of the NSX's upper and lower A-arm suspensions and what many consider the jewel in the NSX's crown, its 24-valve, twin-cam V-6 engine.

Like Ferrari, Honda's reputation began with its engines. And it continues with the NSX V-6—complete with its titanium connecting rods—which comes in two forms. Opt for the six-speed manual gearbox and your V-6 would have 3.2 liters, 290 horsepower, and 224 lb-ft of torque . . . and 0 to 60 in 5 seconds through the very sweet shifter. Choose the four-speed SportShift automatic and its steering wheel-mounted shift levers and you'll have the 3.0-liter V-6 with 252 horsepower and 210 lb-ft of torque. The truly dedicated could, of course, contact Comptech U.S.A., the unofficial NSX racing team for American Honda, and investigate its supercharged, 425-horsepower NSX engine.

What Honda did with the Acura NSX that other exotic carmakers had not managed was to make a fast, mid-engine car that could be enjoyed on a track like a race car, or driven day-to-day as you would any high-quality car.

ACURA NSX-T

Base price: $84,000

Specifications

General

Layout	mid-engine, rear drive
Wheelbase (in.)	99.6
Overall length (in.)	174.2
Overall width (in.)	71.3
Overall height (in.)	46.1
Curb weight (lbs.)	3,090

Drivetrain

Engine	dohc 24-valve V-6
Bore x stroke (mm)	93.0x78.0
Displacement (cc)	3,179
Horsepower	290 bhp @ 7,100 rpm
Torque	224 lb-ft @ 5,500 rpm
Transmission	six-speed manual

Body & Chassis

Front suspension	upper and lower A-arms, compliance pivots, coil springs, tube shocks, anti-roll bar
Rear suspension	upper and lower A-arms, coil springs, tube shocks, anti-roll bar
Steering	rack and pinion, variable electric assist
Brakes	11.7-inch vented discs front, 11.9-inch vented discs rear, ABS
Wheels	16x7 front, 17x8-1/2 rear
Tires	215/45ZR-16 front, 245/40ZR-17 rear

Performance

0 to 60 mph	5.0 seconds
Top speed	168 mph (estimated)

Acura's NSX V-6 has been through several updates and is now sold in two forms. With the manual transmission you get a 3.2-liter, 290-horsepower version of the engine, while the automatic gearbox is matched to a 3.0-liter, 252-horsepower model.

There is nothing wrong with wanting to play Formula 1 driver with the automatic, but in an automobile already so inherently smooth to drive, the manual is really more fun. With traction control on, the NSX is a sweet, safe car to hustle down any twisting road. Turn off the traction control and the NSX takes on a slightly different character, one mastered by your right foot, which now has more control over the car's rear end. In either case, the NSX rides better than most exotic cars and leaves you with a wonderful sense of the road rushing below you.

And you will be in comfort, with seats that hold you in place, good outward visibility, room for an amazing amount of luggage, and, with the 19-pound aluminum targa panel stowed in back, the wind whistling through your hair.

Best yet, the NSX is a relative bargain, priced just above the better Porsche 911s and well below the entry-level Ferrari.

NISSAN R390 GT1

Nissan's R390 GT1 is one of several exotic cars with an important difference: it wasn't really meant to be sold to the public... and how much more exotic can a car get than to be impossible to buy?

Here's what happened. In the late 1990s, the 24 Hours of Le Mans had a class called GT1. To qualify for the class, a car builder was required to create a street-ready machine that could be sold. They only had to build one and they didn't really have to sell it, but the car had to meet street-machine regs.

Was Le Mans a strong enough draw to force an automaker to build such a specialized car? Nissan asked its potential customers that question. The company found that

Nissan discovered that among its customers no single race in the world had the attraction of the 24 Hours of Le Mans. To compete in that famous race, the Japanese company developed the R390. *Photo courtesy of Nissan*

Designed by Ian Callum, who also penned the Aston Martin DB7, the R390 was created to race in the GT1 category. The rules for that class required the company to produce a street-legal version of the car, but did not specify how many, so only a handful of R390s were made. *Photo courtesy of Nissan*

while their car-enthusiast customers put Grand Prix racing at the top of their "favorites" list, the general mass of potential Nissan buyers found Le Mans to be the most important race in the world.

So Nissan decided to attack Le Mans with a car called the R390 GT1. That was in the fall of 1996, and they wanted to be ready for Le Mans the following June. It would be a tight timetable for a pure race car, but Nissan had to build at least that one R390 that was certified for the street, even meeting emissions and crash-safety regulations. They needed help.

England's Tom Walkinshaw Racing (or TWR for short) had extensive experience both at Le Mans, where they won with the Mazda and Jaguar teams, and at producing street-legal exotic cars. So, Nissan went to TWR for assistance with the R390.

The plan was that NISMO (Nissan Motorsports International) would provide the engine for the exotic, while TWR would do the actual car.

Drawing from its experience, TWR created a lightweight carbon-fiber chassis complete with upper and lower A-arm suspensions, rack-and-pinion steering, and huge 14-inch vented disc brakes. Bodywork for the Japanese race car was penned by Ian Callum, who also shaped the Aston Martin DB7 and went on to head Jaguar's design studios.

In Japan, NISMO designed and developed the 3.5-liter twin-turbo V-8 planned for the R390. The lightweight engine block was made from magnesium, while the dual overhead cams opened four valves per cylinder. The R390 was powered

The responsibility for developing and building the body and chassis of the Nissan was farmed out to the Le Mans–winning Tom Walkinshaw racing team. This meant TWR had to design everything from the pseudo-street interior to the carbon-fiber chassis. *Photo courtesy of Nissan*

by 550 horsepower at 6,800 rpm and 470 lb-ft of torque at 4,400, and that was steady, reliable power meant to last for an entire 24-hour endurance race. At the back of the V-8 was a six-speed sequential gearbox.

Inside, the R390 was pure race car. You drop down into seats formed by the center structure and side tanks of the carbon-fiber chassis. Ahead is a typical no-nonsense race-car display of instruments with pertinent information. No frills. One should not expect much in the way of sound-deadening.

That was the basic package that Nissan and TWR certified as street worthy so they could run at Le Mans. And they put a customer price on the car, $1 million.

The 2,420-pound R390 certainly had high-dollar performance, with a 0-to-60 time pegged at 3.9 seconds using gearing that would certainly put its top speed well over 200 miles per hour on Le Mans' Mulsanne straight. Or, presumably, any stretch of open freeway the owner with a great deal of ability and/or courage could find. Wouldn't that tick-off the cops?

NISSAN R390 GT1

Base price: $1,000,000

Specifications

General

Layout	mid-engine, rear drive
Wheelbase (in.)	107.1
Overall length (in.)	185.8
Overall width (in.)	78.7
Overall height (in.)	44.9
Curb weight (lbs.)	2,420

Drivetrain

Engine	turbocharged dohc 32-valve V-8
Bore x stroke (mm)	85.0x77.0
Displacement (cc)	3,495
Horsepower	550 bhp @ 6,800 rpm
Torque	470 lb-ft @ 4,400 rpm
Transmission	six-speed sequential

Body & Chassis

Front suspension	upper and lower A-arms, coil springs, tube shocks, anti-roll bar
Rear suspension	upper and lower A-arms, coil springs, tube shocks, anti-roll bar
Steering	rack and pinion
Brakes	14.0-inch vented discs front and rear
Wheels	18x8 front, 19x10 rear
Tires	245/40ZR-18 front, 295/35ZR-19 rear

Performance

0 to 60 mph	3.9 seconds
Top speed	200 mph (estimated)

While the car was created in England, Nissan made the V-8 engine in Japan. The lightweight engine featured a magnesium block, and while its official horsepower was 550, that power was reliable at race speeds throughout the entire 24 Hours of Le Mans. *Photo courtesy of Nissan*

In reality, it was unlikely Nissan would have sold any R390s. They received queries, but not just anyone would be qualified to drive such a potent automobile. Not only was it a purebred race car, but if retuned for ultimate performance instead of endurance, the turbo V-8 had the potential of up to 1,000 horsepower.

Besides, Nissan and TWR were busy prepping the race cars for Le Mans—and very successfully so. The combination of the English firm's experience and the Japanese engine's power and reliability took R390 GT1s to 3rd-, 5th-, 6th-, and 10th-place finishes in the 1997 24 Hours of Le Mans . . . a race in which finishing one car in the top 10 is impressive.

The GT1 rules changed, and in 1999 Nissan ran its Le Mans project with pure prototypes. This really made more sense, but it is fascinating to consider the place of the R390 and other GT1 cars, such as Porsche's, and that brief time when automakers created some of the most exotic cars ever built.

chapter 4

UNITED STATES

Americans love exotic automobiles. The United States has been the major export market for Ferrari, Porsche, and Lamborghini for years, but it doesn't create its own super-exotic cars. The country has long had the talent, the experience, and the materials to do so, and in the 1930s produced great V-12 and V-16 sedans that rivaled anything in the world. But the United States has always had plenty of cheap, reliable horsepower and inexpensive, readily available fuel, so no one had to break the bank to get ground-pounding power and speed.

Men have tried to make American exotics. John DeLorean took a shot with his stainless-steel, mid-engine sports car, but the effort ended in scandal and lawsuits. The best candidate to be the hands-down U.S. exotic car world-beater, the Vector, had heart-pumping styling and all the speed most drivers could ever control but the Vector suffered from years of poor funding and unkept promises, finally meeting a quiet death in rural Florida.

General Motors took several long, hard looks at doing serious mid-engine exotic cars—the Aerovette, the CERV IV—but could never develop the corporate courage (which is to say,

a winning business plan) to go ahead. GM did own Lotus for a time, just as Chrysler had Lamborghini and Ford runs Aston Martin and Jaguar, but U.S. automakers could just never make a case for home-built exotics.

Chevrolet does, however, build a wonderful Corvette, just as Dodge's Viper is a world-beater in its own class. And how about Carroll Shelby's Ford-powered, U.S.-assembled Cobras?

What do they all share? Good old American engines, with two valves per cylinder and pushrods, based on engines used in rather ordinary cars and/or trucks. And their base prices—minus, perhaps, the Cobra—are in line with Detroit's philosophy of offering the most for a low price.

We do have a U.S. tuner industry. If the stock Corvette and Viper aren't enough, men such as Reeves Callaway and John Hennessey will modify one with enough exotic brakes, carbon-fiber panels, horsepower, and performance to go specifications sheet-to-specifications sheet and price-to-price with any automaker in the world.

But if you're waiting for the likes of GM, Ford, or the Chrysler group to build a true exotic car, don't hold your breath.

DODGE VIPER

Dodge's Viper is every red-blooded American kid's dream car. It's the fastback sports car we sketched in our high-school notebooks. The American answer to imported exotic cars, complete with a big-displacement, bags-of-torque pushrod engine, and an exhaust note that puts even an unmuffled Harley-Davidson to shame. And it has a great—if brief—history.

Even before the 1989 Detroit Auto Show we had a hint that something sporty and remarkable was coming from the Chrysler Corporation. Scrambling to spiff up the image of its Dodge Division, the automaker needed something exciting to tickle our imaginations. But lordy, we never expected what they unveiled: a rugged-looking sports car with an aggressive front end that was almost malevolent. The show car's low

Crank that one-piece hood forward and there it is, the long monster V-10 with its 8.0 liters of displacement, 450 horsepower, and 490 lb-ft of torque. Equipped with a six-speed manual gearbox, the Dodge sports car can leap to 60 miles per hour in just 4.4 seconds.

Opposite: The second-generation Viper changes the proportions a bit and swaps the large one-piece front-hinged engine cover for more conventional fenders and hood. This competition car version confirmed that Chrysler would continue racing the Viper, which has been a consistent winner in international events.

stance was emphasized by a long hood meant to cover—for heaven's sake—an 8.0-liter V-10. Dodge promised not only better-than-Corvette performance, but also a reasonable price.

And here was the best part: Dodge delivered everything it promised.

When the Viper went into production in 1992, it created an instant cult, with potential owners lining up at dealerships to be the first in their neighborhood with the Dodge sports car.

Once you have driven a Viper, it's easy to understand why. You slip down and into the Viper, its tall center console snuggling you into the driving position. It's a nicely laid-out cockpit: the tachometer and speedometer are straight ahead, with the other dials spread out to the right. There's nothing delicate, subtle, or snobbish about the Viper interior, and it's easy to get a good solid grip on the controls—all the better for hanging on.

At the key's turn, the big V-10 starts its odd exhaust note rumble. Into first gear, let out the medium-effort clutch, and the Viper eases away. Nail the throttle and the acceleration will flatten you in the seat, ready to put you back there again when you've hauled it into second gear. In just 4.4 seconds you are at 60 miles per hour, with 100 coming up in 9.8. Top speed? How about 185 miles per hour at the end of the rocket ride?

Okay, it wasn't a perfect car, and could be a bit of a rough-and-ready drive. The cockpit could be hot inside on a summer's day. The original folding soft top was difficult to use and the side curtains leaked when it rained, but these were all minor inconveniences . . . and they were eventually fixed.

At the 1993 Detroit show, Dodge presented the Viper GTS coupe. Not only did the fastback bring the possibility of comfortable all-weather driving, but it also meant even the roadster inherited the badly needed glass side windows.

The Viper's handling also went through a bit of taming. With all that torque and acceleration, the sports car may be nice and stable, but you can easily take to the edge when driving, and just a little brain fade could slide you over the edge. So you have to use your noggin, but the Viper can also be quite predictable as you use the throttle to measure out just how much you want the back end hanging out.

You don't have to stop at stock Vipers. Several aftermarket tuners will customize your Viper. Texan John Hennessey is

With the Dodge Viper, Chrysler created the throaty, tire-smoking American sports car young men had been dreaming about. The body shape, with its near-malevolent smiling grille, is a classic of long-hood/short-rear-deck proportions, whether it is the removable-top sports version or the closed GT with its kicked-up rear spoiler.

The Viper cockpit is divided into two very separate seating areas by the transmission's tall, wide center console. There is a soft, rounded, welcoming sense to the interior, almost a bit deceiving given the car's super performance.

one of the best at making even faster Vipers with such creations as the Venom 650R. After banging out the V-10 to 8.4 liters and giving it the speed treatment, Hennessey's hot rod Viper adds 200 horsepower for a total of 650. But that can be just a beginning, topping an option list that includes the hidden (Brembo brakes and suspension mods), the almost hypnotic (functional aero packages and eye-popping colors), and the expensive (a final price that would buy you a Ferrari 360 Modena). But the hopped-up Viper will also get you to 60 miles per hour in 3.7 seconds and through the quarter-mile in 11.5 seconds at almost 130 miles per hour.

To its credit, Chrysler also wasn't afraid to put the Viper into serious road racing circles. And it went after the international crowd, winning three successive FIA GT2 championships, nailing down class wins in such famous races as the 24 Hours of Le Mans. Chrysler's finest hour was taking an overall victory in the 2000 24 Hours of Daytona.

The Viper is everything we imagined when we were sketching that dream car in our high-school notes and thinking, "What would happen if . . ."

DODGE VIPER

Base price:	$70,000

Specifications

General

Layout	front engine, rear drive
Wheelbase (in.)	96.2
Overall length (in.)	176.7
Overall width (in.)	75.7
Overall height (in.)	47.0
Curb weight (lbs.)	3,380

Drivetrain

Engine	ohv V-10
Bore x stroke (mm)	101.6x98.5
Displacement (cc)	7,990
Horsepower	450 bhp @ 5,200 rpm
Torque	490 lb-ft @ 3,700 rpm
Transmission	six-speed manual

Body & Chassis

Front suspension	unequal-length upper and lower A-arms, coil springs, tube shocks, anti-roll bar
Rear suspension	unequal-length upper and lower A-arms, coil springs, tube shocks, anti-roll bar
Steering	rack and pinion, power assist
Brakes	13.0-inch vented discs front and rear
Wheels	17x10 front, 17x13 rear
Tires	275/40ZR-17 front, 335/35ZR-17 rear

Performance

0 to 60 mph	4.4 seconds
Top speed	185 mph

CALLAWAY C12

It looks like it belongs on a race track. Low and liquid-smooth, the bodywork implies the Callaway C12 sticks to the road like a ground-effects race car. Judging by *Road & Track*'s testing, it comes close to that mark, being one of the rare cars that can generate more than 1.0g of lateral acceleration on a skid pad. Point the C12 straight down the road, however, and it becomes a dragster, the speedo needle whipping past 60 miles per hour in just 4.7 seconds and the 100-mile-per-hour mark just 5.1 seconds later—quick and yet comfortable.

That's the way Reeves Callaway likes his cars.

We first heard from Callaway in 1978, when he began creating turbocharged 3-Series BMWs in a building out in the woods near Old Lyme, Connecticut. Emissions rules had sucked power from automobiles back then, and guys like

When building an automobile that bears his name, Reeves Callaway begins with a stock Corvette. Underneath he adds a modified suspension designed and made in Germany.

The famous small-block Chevrolet V-8 is heavily modified at the Callaway factory in Old Lyme, Connecticut. Among other changes, the cylinder heads and pistons are reworked to modify the combustion chamber shape, and the camshaft profiles are altered. The result is 440 bhp and 420 lb-ft of torque.

Callaway were pumping it back in with turbos. Next came turboed Volkswagens and Porsche 924s that were so impressive because of their added power and superb workmanship that Alfa Romeo hired Callaway to breathe life into its GT6 model. One of these official factory Alfas ended up at General Motors' Milford proving grounds and mightily impressed Dave McLellan's Corvette development group. In 1985, Callaway received the official corporate blessing—an unusual divine approval from GM—to modify Corvettes. He has being doing just that ever since.

When Chevrolet produced the C5 Corvette with its greatly improved chassis and powertrain, it gave Callaway a chance to take an even greater step toward creating more than just modified Corvettes. Although his cars are Corvettes legally converted to conform to the government's emissions and safety rules, there is little in the C12's outward appearance to hint at this heritage. In fact, in Europe the cars are registered as Callaways.

Here's why:

A C12 begins as a set of Corvette bones in Callaway's Leingarten, Germany, factory. Bolted to the 'Vette's stout perimeter frame are new suspensions, upper and lower A-arms developed and hand-fabricated by Munich, Germany's, IVM Engineering. Coil springs/adjustable shock units supplement the stock transverse plastic spring. On go 14-inch-diameter disc brakes, which will later be surrounded by P295/30ZR-19 Pirelli P-Zero tires.

Around this new chassis is custom bodywork designed by Canadian Paul Deutschman and made of fiberglass, carbon fiber, and Kevlar. It's Deutschman who gives Callaways their sleek aero shape, a magic he applies to any of three C12 versions: a fixed-top coupe, a hardtop with a removable central roof panel, and a convertible, which becomes the Speedster model, featuring a unique rear deck lid with headrests.

Callaway also changes the Corvette interior to suit the new exterior. The standard seats are swapped for custom buckets made by Koenig. Like the dashboard, door panels, and center console, the seats are upholstered in a leather of the customer's choice from a wide variety of colors. Custom gauge faces are added, while their surround and parts of the center console get carbon-fiber coverings.

Next comes a trip back to the United States, to Old Lyme for a new engine. The power boffins in the engine shop are world-renowned for their tuning work, having been contracted by Aston Martin to update its V-8 and GM's Holden of Australia to modify the corporation's LT1 V-8s for its Commodore coupes.

For the C12's aluminum Corvette V-8, the shop blueprints the engine and does some serious reworking such as

To finish off the conversion, the company adds custom body panels designed by Canadian Paul Deutschman. With the bodywork arcing out over huge tires, the Callaway C12 takes on a nasty, sit-down-and-shut-up demeanor.

Callaway also modifies the interior of his C12s, with seats custom upholstered from a wide range of leather colors. There are new instrument faces, and the gauges and switches are now set in carbon-fiber accent panels.

machining the heads and pistons to create a new combustion chamber shape, changing the cam profiles, and swapping such stock parts as con rods for beefier pieces. The results were 440 horsepower at 6,300 rpm and 420 lb-ft of torque at 4,800 rpm versus the stock Corvette's 345 horsepower at 5,600 rpm and 350 lb-ft at 4,400 rpm.

Once the buffed-up V-8 is put back in the C12 and bolted to the Corvette's rugged six-speed manual transmission, Reeves Callaway takes the new C12 for a shakedown drive. This is just the sort of personal attention Callaway gives his new cars . . . and what a customer expects when he pays $170,000 to $220,000 for an automobile.

What his money buys is a truly custom-built car. As that price spread implies, there's a lot you can do to personalize your C12. Every C12 owner, however, gets an almost-race car. It has the looks. It has the power. It has the handling. Thankfully it also has an interior that coddles just enough and a surprisingly smooth ride that won't rattle your back teeth.

That's the way Reeves Callaway likes his cars.

CALLAWAY C12

Base price:	$178,500

Specifications
General

Layout	front engine, rear drive
Wheelbase (in.)	104.5
Overall length (in.)	191.0
Overall width (in.)	78.7
Overall height (in.)	47.1
Curb weight (lbs.)	3,380 (estimated)

Drivetrain

Engine	ohv V-8
Bore x stroke (mm)	99.0x92.0
Displacement (cc)	5,666
Horsepower	440 bhp @ 6,300 rpm
Torque	420 lb-ft @ 4,800 rpm
Transmission	six-speed manual

Body & Chassis

Front suspension	upper and lower A-arms, transverse composite monoleaf spring, coil springs, tube shocks, anti-roll bar
Rear suspension	upper and lower A-arms, transverse composite monoleaf spring, coil springs, tube shocks, anti-roll bar
Steering	rack and pinion, variable power assist
Brakes	14.0-inch vented discs front, 11.8-inch vented discs rear, ABS
Wheels	19x10-1/2
Tires	P295/30ZR-19

Performance

0 to 60 mph	4.7 seconds
Top speed	200 mph (estimated)

CHEVROLET CORVETTE C5

If this book had been written before the debut of the fifth-generation Corvette, Chevrolet's sports car would not have been included. There have been great Corvettes, such as the original Sting Rays, but the fourth iteration in this line of fiberglass sports car was not among them. So why is the "C5" included? Because project engineer Dave Hill and his Corvette development team took virtually all the complaints made about the previous generation 'Vette and fixed them.

In creating the Corvette C5, Chevrolet put itself back on the supercar map. No, it's not as exotic as a Ferrari or Lamborghini, but the 'Vette provides almost all their performance at a fraction of their price . . . an exotic car for the working person.

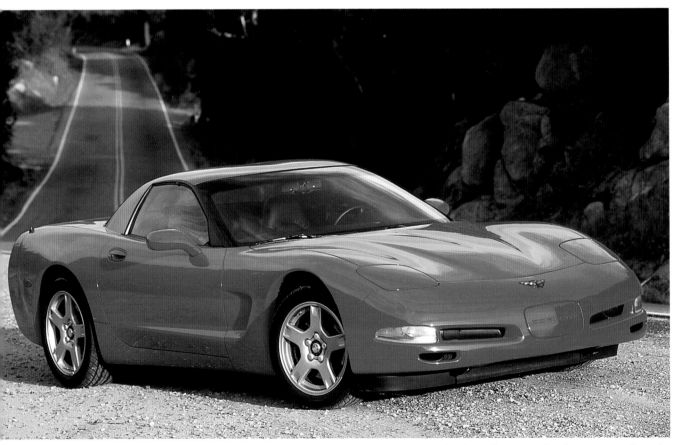

With its fifth-generation Corvette, Chevrolet put itself back in the high-performance big leagues . . . though at a minor league price. The body design updated traditional Corvette styling themes with a hint of Callaway thrown in with the tall rear end shape.

Chevrolet began C5 development by redesigning and dramatically stiffening the chassis of the Corvette with such elements as a new steel perimeter frame, an enclosed transmission tunnel, and lightweight crossbraces. Not only did this create a "stiffer" Corvette, but it gave the chassis engineers a better base for the upper and lower A-arm suspensions at each end of the car, the variable-effort rack-and-pinion steering, and the huge disc brakes.

To power the C5 Corvette, engineers created a new engine wrapped around an old philosophy. They kept the fundamentals of the old V-8—the two-valve-per-cylinder pushrod design, 5.7-liter displacement and cylinder bore centers—integrating them into an all-new aluminum powerplant. It's a typically strong GM small-block engine, with 345 horsepower plus 350 lb-ft of torque that will entertain you from 1,500 rpm right up to the 6,000-rpm redline.

Repackaging the interior created a 'Vette that is a pleasure to live with, where previous Corvettes were not. Entry and exit are now easy. The leather seats are like a gentle hand in the center of your back. Controls are well placed and with a nice touch.

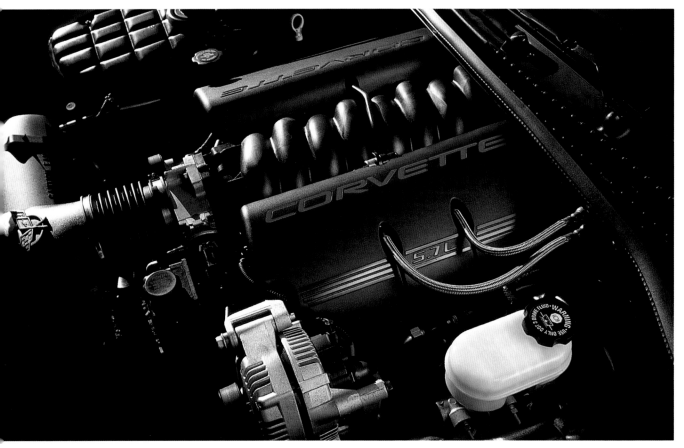

A complete redesign of the small-block V-8 kept traditional elements such as the 5.7-liter displacement and pushrod valve actuation, but advanced the legendary powerplant into the twenty-first century. The all-aluminum fuel-injected engine produces 345 horsepower and 350 lb-ft of low-down torque; manual and automatic transmissions are available.

As a further aid to the chassis engineers, the transmission is part of a rear-mounted transaxle, which led to a 50 front/50 rear-weight balance for the 'Vette.

Designers in the Corvette studio had their chance to clothe the C5 in a new shape. Their efforts took some initial hits from the press, which was looking for something more dramatic. Like many good designs, however, this Corvette quickly became an attractive addition to the sports car ranks. It is also an aerodynamically impressive package, beginning with its low nose and climbing to the tall cut-off tail, producing a 0.29 drag coefficient along the way.

Redesigning created an interior "package" that is much more livable than in past Corvettes. Entry is easy now, no longer requiring you to fall into the seats. The driver and passenger have plenty of room for their heads and elbows. Feet get a break too, as the rear-mounted transmission opens up significant inches of foot room.

Hints of the original Sting Ray's dashboard are the basis for the new layout. Excellent gauges, good controls, and even neat-looking aluminum pedals. Seats that both cushion and support. A very livable cockpit for short spurts or the long haul . . . and a large, usable trunk.

These impressive changes show up in three Corvette models, beginning with the coupe with its removable roof panel for half-open "Targa" driving. The second version of the C5 is the coupe with the fixed top. The third variation is the

Where the fourth-generation Corvette's instrument panel was a disaster, the current model's is an example of how it should be done. The white-on-black gauges are easy to read in high or low light . . . and isn't it a treat to watch that speedo needle twist past 100 miles per hour and keep on swinging?

convertible, where the progress on the C5's chassis and body are most obvious. Quite simply, the last-generation 'Vette's ragtops were rattletraps and the C5s are not. I've been in one with more than 8,000 miles that took on bumpy Michigan secondary road railroad crossings with nary a rattle or a squeak. And the Corvette's top can be put up or down in seconds even though it's a manual with one of the few faults in the new 'Vette: it leaks in heavy rain.

The V-8 rumbles nicely at idle as if waiting impatiently for you to get on with it. Smoothly shift into the first of six gears—or "D" if you prefer the four-speed automatic—and in less than 5 seconds you can be at 60 miles per hour. Another 6.5 seconds and you're at 100 miles per hour.

But there's more than slap-back-in-the-seat acceleration. Despite its price, the Corvette holds its own with megabuck exotics on twisty roads. There's the comfort of initial understeer, but a competent driver can use the throttle to balance the car with the pedal.

So there you have it: an exotic car with value—performance for a price—good looks, a practical interior package, and a proud racing heritage. Proof that you don't have to mortgage your soul to buy a good time in a fast two-seat sports car.

CHEVROLET CORVETTE C5

Base price: $39,000

Specifications
General

Layout	front engine, rear drive
Wheelbase (in.)	104.5
Overall length (in.)	179.7
Overall width (in.)	73.6
Overall height (in.)	47.7
Curb weight (lbs.)	3,230

Drivetrain

Engine	ohv V-8
Bore x stroke (mm)	99.0x92.0
Displacement (cc)	5,666
Horsepower	345 bhp @ 5,600 rpm
Torque	350 lb-ft @ 4,400 rpm
Transmission	six-speed manual

Body & Chassis

Front suspension	upper and lower A-arms, transverse composite monoleaf spring, tube shocks, anti-roll bar
Rear suspension	upper and lower A-arms, transverse composite monoleaf spring, tube shocks, anti-roll bar
Steering	rack and pinion, variable power assist
Brakes	12.8-inch vented discs front, 12.0-inch vented discs rear, ABS
Wheels	17x8-1/2 front, 18x9-1/2 rear
Tires	P245/45ZR-17 front, P275/40ZR-17 rear

Performance

0 to 60 mph	4.8 seconds
Top speed	170 mph

SALEEN S7

Enzo Ferrari. Ferruccio Lamborghini. Steve Saleen?

Why not?

You should know all three names: the first two for their exotic cars, the last for the super Mustangs he has built for the past 17 years, but what do they have in common?

Now they are all exotic car builders. Saleen joins the elite corps with his mid-engine, $375,000 S7.

Unlike Ferrari, Lamborghini, Pagani, and Maserati, Saleen doesn't build his supercar in the greater Modena, Italy, environs, but in rather more prosaic Irvine, California.

Located about 50 miles south of Los Angeles, Irvine is an international automotive center, boasting design studios for Mazda, Mercedes-Benz, and Italdesign, plus the offices of many aftermarket suppliers. It is also the site of the world

Racer and businessman Steve Saleen made his reputation modifying Mustangs, but became a full-fledged automaker with the S7 supercar, which costs $375,000, gets to 60 miles per hour in under 4 seconds, and tops out at over 200 miles per hour.

headquarters for Ford's Prestige Automotive Group, including Jaguar, Land Rover, Aston Martin, and Lincoln.

Dramatically styled with a world-record automotive gill count on its long-tail body, the Saleen S7's design nicely splits the visual difference between road and race car. At 188 inches long, 78.3 inches wide, and 41 inches high, the S7 is a dozen inches longer but 2.5 inches lower than a Lamborghini Diablo and has front-hinged swing-up doors similar to the Italian cars.

Designer Phil Frank did the pen work on the S7, with the aerodynamics tuned and confirmed in the wind tunnel of the University of Glasgow in Scotland.

Why use a tunnel so far from Irvine? The prototype S7 got some engineering assistance from and was built by Ray Mallock's well-known race firm in England. Mallock assembles S7s meant for Europe and the Middle East, with the rest of the world's Saleens being made in Irvine.

While the "S" in the name stands for Saleen, the "7" is for the number of liters in the purpose-built V-8. Although the pushrod engine starts with pieces from Ford's race program, there's a lot of Saleen in there too. For example, the aluminum block is from Ford's race parts catalog, but for packaging reasons has been reworked 8 inches shorter thanks to custom bits

Longer and lower than a Lamborghini Diablo, the S7's wind tunnel–tested bodywork is made of carbon fiber. Under the stunning shape is a tube frame reinforced with aluminum honeycomb panels. The chassis is typical of great exotic cars, with upper and lower A-arm suspensions and Brembo ventilated disc brakes.

For the S7's engine, Saleen engineers begin with an aluminum block from Ford's racing department and highly modify it to 550 horsepower and 520 lb-ft of torque. The dry-sump powerplant features an intake manifold and throttle body made of magnesium and a carbon-fiber air intake.

such as a side-mounted water pump. Among other Saleen pieces are the magnesium intake manifold and throttle body, and the aluminum cylinder heads. Behind the dry-sump V-8 is a six-speed manual transaxle.

Here are the important numbers performance car fans want next: 550 brake horsepower at 6,400 rpm, 520 lb-ft of torque at 4,000 rpm, 0 to 60 miles per hour in under 4 seconds, and a 200+-mile-per-hour top speed, thanks in part to a curb weight of only 2,750 pounds, split 40 percent front/60 percent rear.

Saleen gets that weight to some 600 pounds less than a rear-wheel-drive Diablo, thanks to lightweight chassis construction. The tube frame is supplemented with honeycomb aluminum panels that add rigidity and form front and rear crash safety boxes. Over this goes the carbon-fiber bodywork.

Connolly leather-covered seats sit low in the tub, the driver's set more to the car's centerline, giving the driver a more central driving location and the passenger less of a clamber in over the sill. Instrumentation is simple and rather elegant in its leather-brushed aluminum-and-body-color background. Rearward viewing is by video.

Chassis specs for the S7 are what we would expect from a world-class exotic car. Both the front and rear suspensions use upper and lower A-arms with tube shocks and coil springs.

The interior of the S7 has an asymmetrical layout, with the driver sitting closer to the car's centerline than does the passenger. Fine English leather covers the seats and sets the tone for the rather elegant interior. There is no inside rearview mirror; the car uses a backward-looking video system instead.

Big Brembo brakes hide inside 19-inch forged alloy wheels wrapped with Pirelli P-Zero tires.

Sounds like a race car, doesn't it? And it can be. Saleen's highly successful race team competes with the S7 against international championship-dominating Dodge Vipers and factory Corvettes.

In the exotic-car world it isn't unusual for new projects such as the Saleen to waste away in the oft-promised-never-delivered Never-Never Land of the badly funded for years before fading away. By contrast, the Saleen almost magically appeared on the market in late 2000, ready for sale.

Part of this magic can be attributed to the funding of Tony Johnson and Hidden Creek Industries, a huge automotive parts manufacturing concern. The Saleen's speed-to-market is the result of advanced computer modeling techniques that rocketed the S7 project from first thoughts to finished cars in the remarkably short time of 18 months.

It's nice to see someone building a true exotic car in California, giving potential buyers an American alternative.

SALEEN S7

Base price:	$375,000

Specifications
General

Layout	front engine, rear drive
Wheelbase (in.)	106.2
Overall length (in.)	188.0
Overall width (in.)	78.3
Overall height (in.)	41.0
Curb weight (lbs.)	2,750

Drivetrain

Engine	ohv V-8
Bore x stroke (mm)	104.8x101.6
Displacement (cc)	7,000
Horsepower	550 bhp @ 6,400 rpm
Torque	520 lb-ft @ 5,000 rpm
Transmission	six-speed manual

Body & Chassis

Front suspension	upper and lower A-arms, coil springs, tube shocks, anti-roll bar
Rear suspension	upper and lower A-arms, coil springs, tube shocks, anti-roll bar
Steering	rack and pinion
Brakes	15.0-inch vented discs front, 14.0-inch vented discs rear, ABS
Wheels	19x9-1/2 front, 19x13 rear
Tires	275/30ZR-19 front, 335/25ZR-19 rear

Performance

0 to 60 mph	under 4.0 seconds
Top speed	more than 200 mph

chapter 5

GREAT BRITAIN

The best way to understand and appreciate a modern British supercar is to drive an old British supercar. While heritage tends to play an important role with all the builders of exotic cars, it never seems to show through quite the way it does in Great Britain.

A definite straight line can be drawn from Jaguar's famous Le Mans–winning C- and D-Type race cars of the 1950s forward to the 1990s mid-engine XJ220. That vein of history continues right on to the twenty-first century with the XK180 and F-Type Jaguar show cars, unaffected by the fact that these firms are now owned by Ford . . . that's the momentum of British heritage.

An Aston Martin DBS3 or DBR1 racer—also from the 1950s—is the obvious father of the famed DB4GT (James Bond's car), which begot the Aston V8 GTs that eventually led to the Virage and the thinking that led to the modern DB7.

Again it is this matter of heritage, cars so British through-and-through that even if the DB7 began as a Jaguar and was reengineered into an Aston, it still fits in the pattern.

Drive an old Lotus Elite, an Elan, or a Europa—very lightweight, small four-cylinder engine, fiberglass body—and you'll come to understand the ancestry of the 2000 Lotus Turbo Esprit even as it is sold today with a high-horsepower V-8.

You also need to drive these British supercars on British roads. Not broad, booming German autobahns, but the narrow, twisting, hedge-lined roads that are just a few miles from England's exotic car centers, such as Newport Pagnell, Hethel, and Coventry. Like their history, these lanes of macadam are an influential part of English exotic cars.

It's said there will always be an England, and, thankfully, that means there will always be a Jaguar, an Aston Martin, and a Lotus.

MCLAREN F1

During his years as a successful designer of Grand Prix cars, Gordon Murray was famous for his thoughtful and innovative race cars. So, when the engineer turned away from Formula 1 racing and designed an exotic automobile, it only stood to reason that it would be an equally intelligent machine.

Hence, the McLaren F1—what might be termed the Einstein of the exotics.

Peter Stevens gets credit for the shape of the McLaren, which is notable for being different from other exotic cars. Generally, supercars appear to be broad-shouldered and a bit flamboyant with front and rear spoilers designed to

Thanks to lightweight construction, the F1 weighs in at just over 2,800 pounds and, thanks to the BMW power, gets to 60 miles per hour in just 3.4 seconds, through 100 miles per hour in 7.7 seconds, and on to a top speed of more than 225 miles per hour.

Opposite: McLaren's F1 might be called the "thinking man's exotic car" thanks to the fact that it was designed by automotive engineering genius Gordon Murray. The exterior design was created to provide a top speed in excess of 200 miles per hour and yet keep the F1 stable with no external wings or other spoilers.

add downforce or, in some cases, to add to the "ohh and ahh" factor.

That's not what Murray had in mind. The engineer didn't want his exotic cluttered with add-on aerodynamic devices, so he included them inside the automobile. Instead of being pushed down on the road by air passing over external wings and front lip spoilers, the McLaren is basically pulled down to the road by air channeled under it through a ground-effects undertray diffuser.

There's more to it than that, of course, like a little rear spoiler that pops up during high-speed braking to help keep the aerodynamic center of pressure in balance . . . all of which is leaps and bounds ahead of the simple spoilers that often seem to clutter the exterior of otherwise artful-looking exotic cars.

Murray-thought continues inside, where you find the driver in a seat that is in the middle of the car and somewhat ahead of the passenger seats. There is a variety of reasons for this position. One is to provide a GP driver's perspective when driving. Another is to have the straight-ahead seating-pedal-steering-and-instrument layout of a single-seater, which is almost impossible to achieve in a normal mid-engine exotic.

It's a bit of a step into the driver's seat, but then you settle down cockpit-style, feeling a bit like a fighter pilot. The detailing is superb, like the light gauge faces, the high-tech sound system controls in the center console, the machined pedals, and a red starter button under its flip-up safety cover. No wonder you feel like a jet pilot.

With the passengers sitting to the side and slightly back from the driver, they get an unusual view of the world, one that leaves them feeling slightly vulnerable. Behind the passengers and ahead of the rear wheels are small luggage compartments.

While Williams may be BMW's newest partner in GP racing, their first time around was with Brabham, where Murray was chief designer. So, the engineer went back to his former partners for the engine for his exotic car.

In his talks with BMW, Murray asked for a lightweight, non-turbocharged powerplant that would put out at least 550 horsepower. The company's compact 60-degree V-12 was the logical basis, and engineer Paul Rosche—who worked with Murray in the GP days—led the project. The displacement of the aluminum V-12 is 6.1 liters, and it has such expected features as dual camshafts on each cylinder head, four valves per cylinder, and all the latest electronic engine controls.

What is unusual is the fact that such a large-displacement engine produces not the 550 horsepower or 90.2 horsepower per-liter requested by Murray, but 627 or an impressive 102.8

Gordon Murray asked BMW for a 550-horsepower V-12 to power the new exotic car, but the German automaker managed to coax 627 horsepower and 479 lb-ft of torque from the 6.1-liter, 48-valve powerplant.

Among the unusual features of the McLaren is three-across seating with the driver in the middle. The layout makes it more difficult to get in, but being on the centerline gives the driver more of an open-wheel driving experience.

horsepower from each liter. And there's plenty of torque, too, 479 lb-ft available from 4,000 to 7,000 rpm, which is just 500 rpm shy of the redline. Behind the BMW is a six-speed manual gearbox feeding the rear wheels.

Under the skin are upper and lower A-arm suspensions, with rack-and-pinion steering and brakes with no power assist. The McLaren has vented, cross-drilled discs, with the rears fed extra cooling air during high-speed braking.

With Murray's emphasis on saving weight, the F1 scales in at only 2,840 pounds, meaning it is 1.1 inch longer than a Ruf CTR, but weighs 350 pounds less. With that heavy-duty BMW power, a McLaren in U.S. trim gets to 60 miles per hour in 3.4 seconds, to 100 miles per hour in a mere 7.7 seconds, and—if you have the courage and plenty of road—a top speed of some 230 miles per hour.

Although the exotic-car market collapsed after its debut, the McLaren F1 sold out its entire production run of 100. The car was never meant to be sold in the United States, but was eventually put through a rigorous compliance program by Dick Fritz's Ameritech company. While a basic McLaren F1 cost only $890,000, the price of making the car U.S. Feds-ready added $160,000 plus the owner had to pay an $81,120 gas-guzzler tax.

Hey, it's only money.

MCLAREN F1
(U.S. Specification)

Base price:	$890,000 (As certified for sale in the United States)

Specifications

General

Layout	mid-engine, rear drive
Wheelbase (in.)	107.0
Overall length (in.)	168.8
Overall width (in.)	71.6
Overall height (in.)	44.9
Curb weight (lbs.)	2,840

Drivetrain

Engine	dohc 48-valve V-12
Bore x stroke (mm)	86.0x87.0
Displacement (cc)	6,064
Horsepower	627 bhp @ 7,400 rpm
Torque	479 lb-ft @ 4,000 rpm
Transmission	six-speed manual

Body & Chassis

Front suspension	unequal-length upper and lower A-arms, coil springs, tube shocks, anti-roll bar
Rear suspension	unequal-length upper and lower A-arms, coil springs, tube shocks, anti-roll bar
Steering	rack and pinion
Brakes	13.1-inch vented discs front, 12.0-inch vented discs rear
Wheels	17x9 front, 17x11-1/2 rear
Tires	235/45ZR-17 front, 315/45ZR-17 rear

Performance

0 to 60 mph	3.4 seconds
Top speed	230 mph

ASTON MARTIN DB7 VANTAGE

Newport Pagnell is about two hours north of London, and if you drive down its main street into town from the motorway, you can't miss Aston Martin. Set in red brick buildings on both sides of the road, it looks like a movie set for Ye Olde English Motor Manufacturer.

Aston is perhaps the most quaint-looking exotic car-maker in the world, but don't be fooled. This vest-pocket-sized division of the Ford Motor Company builds one of the most delightfully deceiving supercars on the planet. Not in Newport Pagnell, but just outside the small city of Banbury. There, in

An important part of every British exotic car is its heritage. Aston Martin's V-12-powered DB7 convertible in the foreground is a direct descendent of the company's famous DBR1 race car, which won the 24 Hours of Le Mans in 1959. With the DBR1 in the background are its winning drivers, Carroll Shelby (right) and Roy Salvadori.

As in all Astons, the DB7 features Connolly leather upholstery and Wilton carpeting. While there is a standard palette of colors for the car's exterior paint and interior appointments, the automaker will customize customers' cars to their every wish.

the former mill made modern to assemble Jaguar XJ220s, Aston makes DB7 Vantages.

It didn't start out to be an Aston. Originally, the chassis was developed by another Ford division, Jaguar, as its coupe. When it was decided the car was too small to be the needed Jag, it was inherited by Aston to become the DB7, and Jaguar went on to create the larger XJS.

When introduced in 1996, the DB7 had a supercharged inline-six and received high praise from the press. The body-work was designed by Ian Callum and beautifully carries on the Aston Martin style and image in both coupe and convert-ible forms. Inside each DB7 is one of those classic English

automobile interiors, with Connolly leather-upholstered seats and just the right array of white-on-black gauges. It is both a comfortable and exciting place for driver and passenger, if a bit tight on space for anyone over 6 feet tall.

One of the few remaining automakers that can custom-build complete cars for its clients, Aston will personally tailor your DB7. Have a favorite color you'd like on the exterior or inside your Aston? Prefer carbon fiber instead of wood on the dash? It's yours for the asking . . . and, of course, the paying.

Standard equipment on every DB7's dashboard is a big red button. Push it when the key is on and you start a power-ful mechanical rush up ahead of you . . the reason why the

Vantage qualifies for a book on exotic cars. In 1999, Aston replaced the supercharged six with the first V-12 used in its automobiles.

The V-12 began as a pair of Ford Duratec V-6s that were then blended and built by another Ford subsidiary, the famous race-engine firm of Cosworth Engineering. As installed in the Vantage, the V-12 has a block and twin-cam heads of aluminum alloy, four valves per cylinder, and all the latest in electronic engine management. Just shy of 6 liters, the V-12 boasts 420 brake horsepower at 6,000 rpm and 400 lb-ft of torque at 5,000 rpm.

Aston offers the Vantage with either the five-speed ZF automatic also used in BMW's 750i or the six-speed manual Dodge fits in its Vipers. Either is acceptable, because with all that horsepower and a remarkably wide torque band—85 percent of that 400 lb-ft is available by 1,500 rpm—even the manual DB7 can almost be driven like an automatic.

It's sweet power that's deceptive in its smoothness, so you have trouble believing the watches when the manual-gearbox DB7 hums to 60 miles per hour in just under 5 seconds. The automatic adds only about 0.2 seconds to that timing.

DB7s can be purchased as either a coupe or convertible, with prices that hover around the $140,000 to $150,000 area. Behind the handsome machines are not only the technical might of Ford, but also decades of history, including wins in the world's most famous sports car races.

ASTON MARTIN DB7 VANTAGE

Base price: $140,000

Specifications

General

Layout	front engine, rear drive
Wheelbase (in.)	102.0
Overall length (in.)	184.7
Overall width (in.)	72.0
Overall height (in.)	50.0
Curb weight (lbs.)	4,118

Drivetrain

Engine	dohc 48-valve V-12
Bore x stroke (mm)	88.2x78.8
Displacement (cc)	5,935
Horsepower	420 bhp @ 6,000 rpm
Torque	400 lb-ft @ 5,000 rpm
Transmission	six-speed manual

Body & Chassis

Front suspension	upper and lower A-arms, coil springs, tube shocks, anti-roll bar
Rear suspension	upper and lower A-arms with longitudinal control arms, coil springs, tube shocks, anti-roll bar
Steering	rack and pinion, power assist
Brakes	14.1-inch vented discs front, 13.1-inch vented discs rear, ABS
Wheels	8x18 front, 9x18 rear
Tires	245/40ZR-18 front, 265/35R-18 rear

Performance

0 to 60 mph	4.9 seconds
Top speed	165 mph (limited)

Aston increased the power of its DB7 by replacing the original supercharged inline-six with a 5,935-cc V-12 that has 420 horsepower and 400 lb-ft of torque. The engine's smooth character deceives you into thinking the car could not possibly get to 60 miles per hour in 4.9 seconds . . . but it does.

To go with the power is an upper and lower A-arm independent suspension at each end of the car. The brakes are huge ventilated discs, and the tires are wide and squat. Aston DB7s aren't the sort of automobiles you expect to ride rough and rumbly even on narrow, high-crowned, English roads, and they do not.

But while the DB7 Vantage may slice smoothly down Britain's famous hedgerow-lined lanes, it won't abandon you when the going gets twisty. Let the roadway cut sharply left or right, or should it suddenly rise or drop out from under you, the Aston stays firmly planted. It may lean a bit more than hard-edged exotics—that goes with the smoother ride—but it will never deceive you.

Aston Martin's DB7 Vantage won't raise the hair on the back of your neck like some exotics. It will not growl or snarl or overtly tempt you to lay twin black streaks of rubber every time you leave a stop sign. Then again, it isn't as demanding as those hard-edged exotics, so you cannot only cover ground at a great rate, but be exhilarated without being exhausted at the end of the road.

JAGUAR XJ220

"It makes sense that a Jaguar XJ220's speedometer reads up to 220 miles per hour, and right now the white needle is just shy of that mark. Davy Jones, whose usual Jaguar seat is an IMSA XJR-14 race car, is strapped into the leather-covered driver's seat next to me. We're a couple of feet this side of what now looks like a solid steel ribbon of double Armco barrier. There are 542 turboed horsepower humming behind us and 8 miles of banked circle arcing ahead . . ."

According to the technicians at Fiat's Nardo high-speed circle in southern Italy, Davy had the Jaguar pegged at 218 to

Some would argue that Jaguar's XJ220 was the sleekest, prettiest supercar from the 1990s. Designer Keith Helfet was responsible for the shape, which takes traditional Jaguar design thinking, from the old D-Type to the sensational mid-engine XJ13 race car, and blends it into a road machine.

220 miles per hour. It was quite a ride I was taking for *Road & Track*, strapped snugly in the passenger's seat wearing a racing suit and helmet, watching Davy make little corrections to allow for minute track imperfections.

And what is the most lasting memory of that high-speed run? That of all the exotic cars of the past two decades, Jaguar's XJ220 was the limousine of the lot. Not a rough-edged, raspy pseudo–race car. Never the twitchy ill-behaving beast. But just the sort of supercar one would expect of the company that has both won the 24 Hours of Le Mans and built decades of comfortable XJ sedans.

Jaguar's XJ220 began as an after-hours project of Jaguar employees led by Director of Product Engineering Jim Randall.

The highly regarded engineer wanted to build a Group B Jaguar a la Porsche 959. Suppliers donated materials. Company designer Keith Helfet, working with studio head Geoff Lawson, contributed the exterior design, while Nick Hull did the interior.

The resulting XJ220 concept car was unveiled at the 1988 Birmingham Show: long, sleek, silver, V-12, four-wheel drive, 200-mile-per-hour top speed . . . and such a hit that Jaguar decided to build the car.

Lacking the manpower and facilities to build a series of mid-engine exotic cars, Jaguar turned the project over to JaguarSport, which it jointly ran with Tom Walkinshaw's TWR.

Developing the XJ200 for production necessitated changes.

Supercar interiors tend to have a more exotic look, but the Jaguar's is elegant . . . as a Jaguar should be. Nick Hull designed the XJ220's interior, including seats that are as speed-worthy as they are sumptuous. To keep the low-roof interior from causing a confining "bunker effect," the roof has a tinted glass panel.

The only disappointment in the XJ220 is its engine. It is certainly powerful enough, with 542 horsepower and 475 lb-ft of torque, but the turbocharged V-6 has a rather agricultural sound and rattle to it. The powerplant is, however, well displayed and viewed through a large glass engine cover.

Sadly, the V-12 had to go, its place taken by a 3.5-liter twin-turbo V-6. The four-wheel drive was replaced with two-wheel drive. The car was shortened by 10 inches in length—8 from the wheelbase—cutting weight some 700 pounds to 3,025 pounds. Shortening the XJ220 did nothing to harm the looks of the XJ220, which has all the beauty and grace expected of a Jaguar . . . plus an aerodynamic drag coefficient of 0.36.

The interior is appropriate to Jaguar's reputation, with the closest thing to comfy overstuffed seats you'll find in a supercar. The full array of gauges includes a few, like the clock and turbo boost gauge, fitted to the door. There are luxuries, such as air conditioning, electric window lifts, and an Alpine stereo with a 6-CD changer. And to keep the low roof from creating a "bunker effect" interior, a smoked glass roof lets in the light.

The turbo V-6 was adapted from Jaguar's XJR-10 and -11 race cars, but traces its history back through the Rover Metro 6R4 rally car. In the super Jag, the dry-sump V-6 has twin cams, four valves per cylinder, and a pair of turbos to produce 542 horsepower at 7,000 rpm and 475 lb-ft of torque. Behind the turbo V-6 is a five-speed manual transmission.

Jaguar's factory for the XJ220 was a converted ancient mill in Bloxham outside Banbury where Aston Martin DB7s would later be made. Inside, it looked like an assembly line of race cars. In one end came chassis tubs made of aluminum honeycomb and paneling. A steel roll cage, upper and lower A-arm suspensions fore and aft, and 90-liter fuel cells were installed. On went AP racing discs brakes with neither power assist nor ABS. Add the drivetrain and aluminum body panels and bolt-on Speedline wheels fitted with Bridgestone Expedia tires.

Out the other end went 350 finished XJ220s . . . to a troubled existence. Between the time when prospective owners—many of them speculating in supercar futures—plunked down $75,000 deposits on the $500,000 Jaguars and the start of production at Bloxham, the market for supercars went in the tank. Buyers backed out, lawsuits flew. Jaguar wasn't able to sell all of its XJ220s until mid-1999. By the end of the century, XJ220s were appreciating back to their original price.

Those who took possession of their XJ200s got what might be the prettiest of the supercars: elegance in a class where racy beauty is the norm. They got precise supercar handling balanced by possibly the smoothest ride in the genre. A rush to 60 miles per hour in the brief span of 3.8 seconds, the V-6 spoiled only by a rattling engine noise that sounds too agricultural.

And an appropriate top speed of 220 . . . just ask me, I've been there.

Previous pages: **Jaguars are supposed to look sleek, and the XJ220 does just that. The acceleration from the 3.5-liter turbo V-6 gets the 3,234-pound supercar to 60 miles per hour in 3.8 seconds, and we can personally attest to the fact the great cat can get to well over 200 miles per hour.**

JAGUAR XJ220

Base price:	$500,000

Specifications

General

Layout	mid-engine, rear drive
Wheelbase (in.)	103.9
Overall length (in.)	194.1
Overall width (in.)	87.4
Overall height (in.)	45.3
Curb weight (lbs.)	3,025

Drivetrain

Engine	turbocharged dohc V-6
Bore x stroke (mm)	94.0x84.0
Displacement (cc)	3,496
Horsepower	542 bhp @ 7,000 rpm
Torque	475 lb-ft @ 4,500 rpm
Transmission	five-speed manual

Body & Chassis

Front suspension	upper and lower A-arms, coil springs, tube shocks, anti-roll bar
Rear suspension	upper and lower A-arms, coil springs, tube shocks, anti-roll bar
Steering	rack and pinion
Brakes	13.0-inch discs front, 11.8-inch discs rear
Wheels	9x17 front, 14x18 rear
Tires	255/45ZR-17 front, 345/35ZR-18 rear

Performance

0 to 60 mph	3.8 seconds
Top speed	220 mph

LOTUS ESPRIT

Among the world's exotic cars, the Lotus Esprit is the grand-daddy. The old man. The survivor. In an automotive world in which everything seems so new and ever changing, the Esprit is, well, no spring chicken.

And yet if you put a new Esprit in about any parking lot in the world, it will draw a crowd of admirers. They aren't interested in the car's history. All they know is that it looks like a supercar . . . and it is.

Famed designer Giorgetto Giugiaro drew the original Esprit show car introduced in 1974, the year the Lamborghini Countach went into production. It was two years before the Esprit was in showrooms, but that still puts its on-sale date

Although it is still an exciting-looking exotic car, the basic Giugiaro-designed shape of the Esprit has been around since 1974, proving that good design is lasting.

two years before Mario Andretti won his Formula 1 championship in a Lotus in 1978.

The original Esprit was a fairly basic car. There was a mid-engine, backbone chassis—a Lotus trademark—with independent suspension front and rear. Power came from the company's 2.0-liter four through a five-speed manual gearbox. The body was formed of fiberglass and smelled of it, so when you worked your way down and into the seat of an early Esprit, there was a certain kit-car aroma to it. Fit and finish were okay, but not up to Ferrari standards.

Lotus founder and designer Colin Chapman was famous for keeping things mechanically simple and light, and the Esprit suffered in some ways for that, at least in the way of finish and amenities.

But what a treat to drive. Light and precise, the Lotus would scamper along the narrow, hedge-lined roads around the company's Hethel, England, factory like a jackrabbit that can quickly and confidently stop, start, jink left, and scamper right, always ahead of the fox.

Over the decades, the Esprit went through many changes. Come 1981 there was a significant power boost with the first Turbo Esprit and its 2.2-liter 210-horsepower turbocharged four. Using some of the money earned when it developed the failed DeLorean gullwing sports car, Lotus upgraded the entire

Under the Esprit's fiberglass body is the classic Lotus backbone frame, with the sort of independent-suspension chassis expected from a company so renowned for its fine-handling automobiles.

Esprits have always been comfortable cars, with the driver nestled in a leather-covered seat between the tall center console and the door. And with the large sunroof, the car has a very open feeling, making the Esprit a delight for a quick, fair-weather drive.

chassis. Within a decade, that same turbo engine would put out some 264 horsepower in the United States.

While the original wedge shape of the Esprit survived, as the car moved though the 1990s, it was modified, made smoother, and filled out in the right places, like a well-trained athlete. So despite its age, the fiberglass-bodied Esprit has remained visually contemporary . . . and has probably the nicest-looking rear wing in the exotic car business.

What really kicked the Lotus in the modern times was the Type 918. That is the company's code name for an all-aluminum V-8 of its own design that debuted in the Esprit in 1996. Don't forget, in addition to being an automaker, Lotus is

famous for its engineering, one example being the Corvette ZR1 V-8.

For its own supercar, Lotus developed a 3,506-cc V-8 with four valves per cylinder and a pair of turbochargers. While most companies go to outside firms for items such as fuel injection and engine management systems, Lotus created its own. And true to the Colin Chapman pursuit of light weight, the entire engine weighs only 485 pounds, "dressed" and ready to install.

In the Esprit with its five-speed manual gearbox, you'll be at 60 miles per hour in 4.4 seconds. Stay in fifth to the redline and you'll see the speedo needle hovering around 178 miles per hour.

At the 1996 Geneva Auto Show, Lotus unveiled the latest engine for the Esprit, a lightweight 3.5-liter, 32-valve, twin-turbo V-8 with 350 horsepower, which is enough to power the car to 60 miles per hour in just 4.4 seconds.

To go with all the added power, Lotus has continually developed the backbone chassis of the Esprit. The front suspension has upper and lower A-arms, while the rear design uses upper and lower transverse links with trailing arms. Brembo ABS disc brakes are inside the alloy wheels fitted with squatty profile Michelin Pilot SX tires.

Lotus hasn't forgotten the interior. Although the fundamental layout is as it was in the late 1970s, this Esprit bears no resemblance to that ancestor, thanks to Connolly leather seats and walnut trim, with sound and air conditioning systems to coddle you.

And at a price in the mid-$80,000s, the Lotus Esprit V-8 is a relative bargain . . . all that luxury and power, but without losing the jackrabbit senses of that original Esprit.

LOTUS ESPRIT

Base price:	$85,250

Specifications

General

Layout	mid-engine, rear drive
Wheelbase (in.)	96.0
Overall length (in.)	172.0
Overall width (in.)	73.5
Overall height (in.)	45.3
Curb weight (lbs.)	3,043

Drivetrain

Engine	dohc 32-valve V-8
Bore x stroke (mm)	83.0x81.0
Displacement (cc)	3,506
Horsepower	350 bhp @ 6,500 rpm
Torque	295 lb-ft @ 4,250 rpm
Transmission	five-speed manual

Body & Chassis

Front suspension	upper and lower A-arms, coil springs, tube shocks, anti-roll bar
Rear suspension	upper and lower transverse links, trailing arms, coil springs, tube shocks, anti-roll bar
Steering	rack and pinion, power assist
Brakes	11.6-inch vented discs front, 11.8-inch vented discs rear, ABS
Wheels	17x8.5 front, 18x10 rear
Tires	235/40R-17 front, 285/35ZR-18 rear

Performance

0 to 60 mph	4.4 seconds
Top speed	178 mph

INDEX